# Colwyn Bay Accredited
# The Wartime Experience

Home of the Headquarters of the Ministry of Food,
and other contributions to the war effort.

### Cindy Lowe

*Colwyn Bay Accredited: The Wartime Experience*
First published in Wales in 2010 on behalf of the author
by
BRIDGE BOOKS
61 Park Avenue
WREXHAM
LL12 7AW


©2010 Cindy Lowe


All Rights Reserved.
No part of this publication may be reproduced,
stored in a retrieval system, or transmitted
in any form or by any means, electronic,
mechanical, photocopying, recording or
otherwise, without the prior permission
of the Copyright holder.


*Cover illustration: Pwllychrochan Hotel from a postcard postmarked 1904,
produced for the Milton Arlette series, N° 135.
by Woolstone Bros, London, EC.*

ISBN 978-1-84494-065-3


A CIP entry for this book is available from the British Library


Printed and bound
by
MWL
Pontypool

*This book is dedicated to:*

*Beryl Lowe Hayes (née Russell)*
*Albert Rigby*
*Captain Harry Parker, RA*

*Who died during the time this book was written.*

*They too loved Colwyn Bay.*

# Contents

| | | |
|---|---|---|
| Preface | | 9 |
| Introduction | | 13 |
| 1 | Food plans under the flight path | 17 |
| 2 | The wider area. Secrets, Safety and Spies | 21 |
| 3 | The town of Colwyn Bay and its particular contribution | 26 |
| 4 | The Ministry of Food. 'Foodtown on Sea' | 34 |
| 5 | Social, Economic and Cultural effects of the influx | 50 |
| 6 | Oral History. Reflections | 61 |
| 7 | Contributions from all over Britain | 98 |
| 8 | The War | 110 |
| 9 | Developments and Impact | 114 |
| 10 | 'Opportunity or Menace'. Does the town now deserve credit and reparation? | 121 |
| Notes | | 124 |
| Bibliography | | 131 |

# Illustrations

| | |
|---|---:|
| *Luftwaffe* flight map | 18 |
| Advert for the Colwyn Bay Fur Company | 26 |
| Members of the LDV drilling, 1940 | 28 |
| Home Guard on parade | 29 |
| Colwyn Bay County School ATC, 1942 | 30–1 |
| Col Llewellin meets the Auxiliaries | 32 |
| Adverts illustrating the range of the Ministry of Food's work | 35 |
| Lord Woolton inspecting members of the Home Guard | 37 |
| Map of the world showing the distances food travelled by sea | 41 |
| Colwyn Bay Hotel | 42 |
| Digging for victory | 43 |
| Metropole Hotel | 45 |
| Copy letter from Lord Woolton thanking staff | 47 |
| Col Barton takes the salute as Auxiliaries march past | 51 |
| Auxiliaries being inspected by Controller Chitty | 52 |
| Jeep assembly line at Braid's Garage | 52 |
| Women working on munitions at Braid's Garage | 54 |
| Completed jeeps parked near Braid's Garage | 55 |
| Count of marriages at St Paul's and St John's churches | 56 |
| TOC H canteen ladies | 57 |
| Classification of occupations of grooms | 58 |
| Certificate of thanks for hosting of evacuees | 62 |
| Class of College School 1942–3 | 69 |
| Albert and Pat Rigby | 76 |
| Typists at Mount Royal Ministry of Food Office | 81 |
| Letter of permission to establish a diamond factory | 91 |
| Examples of machine tools used in the diamond industry | 92 |
| Opening of the diamond factory, 31 July 1941 | 94 |
| Floor plan of diamond factory | 95 |
| Mayor and children at diamond industry exhibition | 96 |

| | |
|---|---:|
| Hans Wins with Mrs Roberts | 96 |
| Frish & Wins personnel | 97 |
| Home Guard on Promenade, Colwyn Bay | 100 |
| Ode to No 10 Pl, B Coy, 11th (Denbighshire) Home Guard | 101 |
| Col Barton taking the salute from Alec Parselle | 102 |
| Letters of congratulation to Alec Parselle | 103 |
| Colwyn Bay Pier | 117 |
| Interior Cartmell Hotel | 120 |

# Preface

I was keen to research this topic ever since I was surprised, delighted and proud to discover that my hometown had been involved in saving the nation from hunger during The Second World War. It had managed this through its efficient organisation and administration as the Headquarters of the Ministry of Food. As a second generation administrator myself, daughter of a civil servant who had worked in those very offices after the war at the 'Metropole' from the first instigation of Social Security, I was fascinated.

It was my mother-in-law Beryl Lowe, (née Russell), who having lived through the war years in Colwyn Bay as a teenager, first told me about the presence of the Ministry during wartime. No one had ever mentioned it to me before, although I was born and bred in Colwyn Bay. When I was growing up there was no conversation about this important role. In wartime my father had enlisted in the RAF and met my mother while training in Cumberland, but they did not settle in Colwyn Bay until after their marriage in 1948. It was then a relatively new town that sprang up as so many with the coming of the railways in the nineteenth century. I have Welsh blood, was born in Colwyn Bay and my father's family, from Denbigh, spoke Welsh as a first language.

I was captivated by the idea of all that went on locally during the war and wanted to know why it was never discussed or given any significance. As I returned from living abroad the Welsh word *Hiraeth* (which has no exact English translation, the nearest thing is homesickness) became meaningful, there is no English equivalent which puts it so succinctly. There is a saying that 'the best Welshman is outside of Wales,' meaning that we most appreciate what we miss. After a teaching career in London I had worked abroad for several years, not returning until I married a local man whom I had known for twenty years, and who was born above Lowe's restaurant, the former Cartmell Hotel central in the town and now the Prince Madoc on Station Road. Of course I always visited my family in the Bay and never lost my links with the town, but returning from afar brought a new perspective.

I wanted to study for a master's degree because I wanted to explore the history of my own local area. Fellow students entered the course not knowing what they would research but I had a topic which was rarely discussed and about which I was passionate. Unfortunately there was little documentation and therefore I was warned against choosing this particular topic for a masters' dissertation because of the lack of available material, also I had to travel from Surrey to Wales to research. I resorted to the use of oral history, about which I was passionate. I was very determined to collect it while I could and eventually found more than I could use.

I am grateful for the help and guidance of Dr Christopher French of Kingston University during my research. At the time I worked full time in a local college and studied, travelling up and down the motorway from Surrey to Colwyn Bay, continuing to amass information and contacts at every opportunity up to the present day and still counting. I started the search for information through reminiscence. It wasn't easy. An expensive advert posted in the North Wales Weekly News one Thursday in the summer of 2006 produced not even one result. It seems that people are happier to be referred by others and perhaps understandably mistrustful of strangers

As my research began in earnest and I began to contact local historical societies the name that cropped up time and again, was that of a local historian, Graham Roberts. I thank him for kindly putting me in touch with one or two residents including his own mother who had been an employee of the Ministry in the war years. He also sent me an obituary of a civil servant who had been responsible for the 'Dig for Victory Campaign.' This book is a result of my research and outlines some of what I discovered on my journey.

Please contribute. If you have any memories of Colwyn Bay which we can record, please contact me through the publisher or through the library at Colwyn Bay.

Many thanks to the staff of Colwyn Bay Library, the Denbighshire Record Office, Ruthin, the Imperial War Museum, London and the National Archives, London. Thanks to my publisher and copy editor Gary Smailes. Finally, and most importantly, I want so much to thank all the contributors to whom I am so grateful for so gladly and enthusiastically sharing their experiences and giving their memories to record for posterity, in particular those who worked at saving the country from hunger in the Second World War.

Cindy Lowe
2010

# Introduction

Never before in its short history had the Victorian seaside resort of Colwyn Bay had such an important role. Yet the extraordinary contribution in housing the staff and manning the Ministry of Food has gone unaccredited. The organisation comprised not only of the sheltered five thousand civil servants but also so many locals, young people and women recruited for employment to form an army of clerks in an insurmountable task. There were so many departments as in a directory compiled by one of the contributors, and they supported the administration, liaising with all the commonwealth countries in the importing of food, which was at risk of being torpedoed at sea en route at any time. Then there were few telephone lines and hardly any paper. What those civil servants and clerks achieved was not far short of miraculous, headed in 1940 by the very pragmatic leadership of Lord Woolton.

Other contributions may be well documented but there was an absence of original evidence about the headquarters of the Ministry of Food. Why had no credit been given? Reminiscence has been used to verify information from various sources, from the first arrival of the civil servants coming to investigate prior to the removal from Whitehall, with the evidence of Mr Albert Rigby at the information bureau, to the evacuation. The people of the town reacted with mixed feeling to the complete change in character of their town, increasing in population by 25% overnight, and requisitioning all available buildings as office space and accommodation.

Some original sources used were Newspapers, Marriage records, Documents of the Ministry of Food in The National Archives, the Imperial War Museum and in Denbighshire Public Records Office at Ruthin Gaol. Oral history evidence supports all of these and locally written books.

The evacuation to Colwyn Bay of the Department of the Ministry of Food is not extensively described in writing, Ivor Wynne Jones describes events succinctly in *Colwyn Bay its History Across the Years*[1] and Geoffrey Edwards in 1984 in a chapter of his book *The Borough of Colwyn Bay. A Social History*.[2] A record of the work of the Ministry was commissioned during the war and archived. It will be shown how oral history is used throughout as confirmation of the effect of events on the town. Where documents are unavailable evidence is a vital source to bridge some gaps as in the case of experiences and work of the civil service at Colwyn Bay during wartime. Too few documents have survived or were destroyed.[3] There was no census during the war years and school logbooks are closed for 75 years.

> Elderly people probably make the best contributors in that they have reached a contemplative stage of their life when they themselves are trying to make sense of their past, and the recording process becomes a natural part of this.[4]

All oral history contributors interviewed were at the time of the interview necessarily between seventy eight and ninety five and would have been between ten years old and in their early twenties during wartime, therefore their memories may be coloured to some extent by a rose tinted view of the past. This may be the only means of locating some information not represented. John Tosh says of oral history – 'Both oral history and oral tradition were initially valued as a means of direct access to the past. Today they are increasingly regarded as evidence of how non-elite communities construct and modify meaning over time.'[5]

Interviews generally took place in private homes, except for one interview in a hospital, and another at a Scout Centenary. Finding contributors proved difficult initially, and an advert in the local press brought no response, neither did notices in doctors' surgeries and charity shops. A mailing was sent to fourteen retirement homes, which brought only two responses, both negative. From one or two known contacts, word of mouth and recommendation produced plentiful results. It seemed from their evidence that half the population of the town had worked at the Ministry of Food in their youth, but how many would be available or willing and able to contribute? A diverse selection of contributors was found through networking, joining the Civic Society, through Friends Reunited and searching blogs about local history. Some contributors had been at school, others temporary clerks, some of whom had made the civil service their career and relocated to Guildford after the war. One lady, now well into her nineties had moved from Saville Row, London as personal assistant to Sir William Duffy, head of the Bread Division. By chance she is the aunt of my partner's first wife. Another, a local girl, was fortunate in finding work at the diamond factory, as her mother had been landlady of the manager; she then went on to work at the Ministry later. This lady had been my mother's best friend since 1948 but had never talked to me about the war years until now. The son of the founder of the diamond factory was first found on a blog then tracked down and encountered visiting the local Scout centenary. Another gentleman also discovered on a blog turned out to have been married to my father's cousin who neither he nor I had ever met, and my father last saw her branch of the family in 1914. So my tenacity and detective work produced some uncanny coincidences and led me to realise how tight knit a community the area had been during wartime, and to an extent still is.

The method of recording oral history was through personal face-to-face interview, except in few cases of telephone interviews long distance. Some photographs from the Denbighshire Record Office in Ruthin and excerpts from the local wartime newspaper stimulated discussion. A set of questions had been prepared, but these were answered in no particular order and the discussion was informal and relaxed, all were enthusiastic. They recommended further contributors and it seemed that there is a close network among the age group. Without an introduction to the circle, collection of material would have been problematic. Initials were sometimes used to preserve anonymity.

In chapter 2, other aspects of the contribution of the surrounding area are taken into account while chapter 3 describes the particular contributions of the town. But the main focus is on the relocation of the Headquarters of the Ministry of Food and all it entailed. Some of the work of the Ministry is discussed in chapter 4 and many of the surviving documents and Cabinet papers at the National Archives have been explored. Apart from a few addresses on letter headings little attention is paid to the venue where all the organisation took place. Some of the changes the upheaval brought as a reception area are parallel to events and changes going on in all other parts of the country such as the effects of the necessary mixing of the classes, observations on which gave rise to the Beveridge Report and the instigation of the Welfare State. Chapter 5 examines the changes brought about, particularly in the lives of women, which were irreversible. A study of marriages of the day at two churches analyses demographic change over wartime. There was disruption to the education system of those children who are now in their eighties and have told their stories. Some fond memories and anecdotes show that there was some humour employed in adversity. The oral history reflections are a small sample of what could be available. Many people had memories or information to share, there is surely much more. It is anticipated that many more people will come forward to volunteer further information of their past, both in this and in every area. Not only are the opinions of the local population represented but also many of the incoming influx of civil servants, and one refugee. A response to a letter in a magazine brought replies from all over the country, which portrayed a fondness for the town and a pride in the valuable achievements of seventy years ago.

Since those days many other families and individuals have arrived to make the town their home. Few will know the extraordinary events which took place, but the evidence recorded and preserved here together with the developments covered since the war will hopefully play a role in informing a future generation who will live happily in the newly regenerated version of Colwyn Bay we hope for.

# 1: Food plans under the flightpath

No weapon ever invented is more deadly than hunger, it can spike guns, destroy courage, and break the will of the most resolute peoples.[6]

At 2am on 7 May 1941, the pilot of a Heinkel 111 leaned over in the cockpit to peer through the perspex at the dark vista below. He was returning from a bombing raid on Liverpool. Below was Wales, the country about which he had been briefed. He had seen the landscape on the approach earlier that night and knew it was mountainous and dangerous terrain. He had heard it rumoured that the *Führer* expected some support in these quarters,[7] and there was currently a process for gathering information.[8] He was exhausted and hungry, desperate to return to base, having dutifully bombed the targets, following the orders of Hugo Sperrle. He would now fly towards the lights on the coast of Eire and then back over France. The bombers would not be jettisoning any unused munitions tonight; his load was already lightened since all had been dropped on Liverpool. He knew it must have caused mayhem but did not realise just how many had been killed or injured this week, nearly two thousand, the worst of the Blitz on Liverpool. As he flew over Colwyn Bay he mused that it would have been wasteful to bomb that imposing building which he had seen nestling under the woods. He knew how the *Führer* liked to preserve good architecture, and how he enjoyed Paris. Hitler had plans for Oxford and Cambridge too. But this town below had never been a target.

The pilot veered upwards and sped on over the Conwy valley, followed by others, ignoring the town below, which they thought of little significance. How wrong they were. What the pilots (or Sperle, Goring and Hitler) did not realise was that the building they had seen below was the old Pwllychrochan Hotel which. along with the two private schools had been converted to one of the main centres of the Ministry of Food headquarters. The Colwyn Bay Hotel, the Metropole and the Queens Hotel housed some of the best scientific advisors and brilliant minds in the

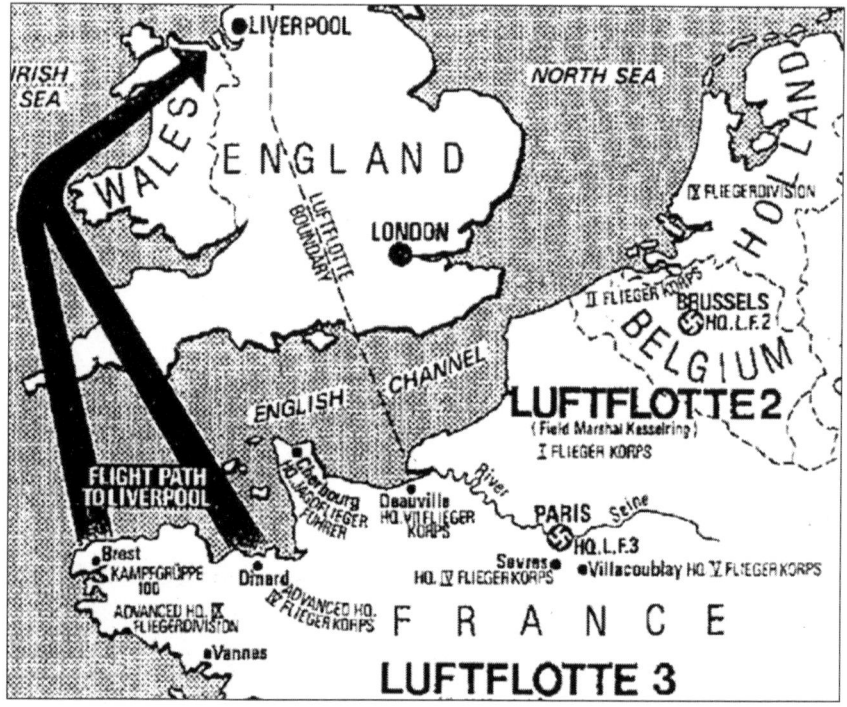

Luftwaffe *flight map*. [NWWN, 25 April 1989]

country. They had recently left Whitehall and assembled there to safely carry out the Food Defence Plans after the town became the Headquarters of the Ministry of Food for Britain in 1940. If these building had been devastated and key staff lost then what … the organisation of the country's food supplies would have been thrown into chaos.

The civil servants, the townspeople, and many Merseyside children lay in their beds below, listening with dread to planes going by, praying that no bombs would fall, wondering what news there would be in the morning. Many had family back in Liverpool, others had fathers who were away fighting, some had already suffered trauma. When the drone of the engines had subsided some of those whose houses overlooked the coast arose trembling in the dark in trepidation, and careful not to let light escape through chinks in the blackout curtains saw from their windows that the sky was red with flames above Merseyside, just across the sea.

The Second World War had a huge impact on North Wales, on the area and its population, with particular reference to the special contribution of Colwyn Bay to the war effort. There was naturally an obvious reward, but also local benefits were bestowed on the town in return for disruption. There was a countrywide expectation of contribution and it was gladly given, but here there was little recognition. The population of North Wales responded, as did every area, appropriately to its geography and economy, either enlisting or contributing in industry or bureaucracy.

It was a well-kept secret, and is still now a lesser known fact, that during The Second World War a government department, The Ministry of Food, was relocated from Whitehall to the town of Colwyn Bay. Under 'The Yellow Move' a total of twenty three thousand civil servants were dispatched to the better coastal resorts and spa towns.[9] Additional hotels in other areas were requisitioned for a possible 'Black move' – in the event of the government fleeing a destroyed capital. In the 'Yellow Move' other ministries and government departments were evacuated, the Ministry of Education to Bournemouth, the Geographical Section (MI4) to Cheltenham and the Inland Revenue to Llandudno, a neighbour of Colwyn Bay. These moves were not only for the safety of the departments, as in the case of food, a nation could obviously not survive without the safety of an efficient organisation of supply and distribution – but another consideration could have been to make more room, required for the cabinet in Whitehall. Five thousand civil servants arrived in Colwyn Bay en masse in September 1940 along with filing cabinets containing names of everyone in the country.[10] Colwyn Bay became the headquarters, necessitating the requisitioning of many buildings for office space and accommodation. There were nineteen divisional offices throughout the country, local offices and buffer depots in every area.

These Food Defence plans were formulated back in 1936 and were based on the experiences of Lords Devenport and Rhonda who had been responsible for food defence plans during the First World War as discussed in chapter 4. All was ready in case war should break out and food supplies threatened. Lack of food would not weaken the population or destroy morale again and what was performed regarding the provision and distribution of food was miraculous, not unlike the 'feeding of the five thousand'. The 'army' of five thousand civil servants was headed by the Manchester businessman Lord Woolton, who applied the lessons of a successful business career (he had set up Lewis' of Liverpool – not connected to John Lewis).[11] While the men of the town had enlisted, housewives, teenagers even older children when on holiday from school, all combined to join the workforce to perform the miracle. As well as the requisition of the Pwllychrochan Hotel, and the two large private schools Rydal and Penrhos, so many of the other buildings were seized and this naturally had a disruptive effect on the town. Many say it never recovered. Yet no credit was ever given for the huge contribution by the people of this small quiet Victorian seaside resort.

'War is a spur to a higher level of social attainment, destroying what is moribund, and bringing out the best qualities in a people.'[12] This quote from *The Benefits of War* a Conservative pamphlet, comments regarding the effect of war on the character of the wartime population, and evidence to reaffirm this is discussed in later chapters by the contributors of oral history. During their interviews specific questions were asked such as:

What was the local contribution of the area to the war effort ?

What was the impact of the war on this area and its population ?

How did the area change because of the war

Was the contribution recognised?

Some events can mirror or be compared to other areas, but certain contributions are unique. Views of the wartime residents derived through oral history interviews have been gathered and can support newspaper editorials describing the effects of the influx. The town was a safe haven for the Ministry with available vacant seasonal accommodation. Families responded to the welfare of evacuees although they may have had little materially themselves. The enclave became a refuge, a quiet relatively peaceful place and this shelter was its greatest contribution. No area was entirely safe, coastal defences were necessarily monitored, neutral Eire was close by and North Wales was directly under the flight path from France to Liverpool. In industry there was prolific assembly of jeeps from parts shipped to Liverpool and manufacture of not only munitions but also diamond tools (used in the production of navigation instruments), both occupations vital contributions to the war and both in which women were active.

## 2: The wider area of North Wales. Safety, secrets and spies

Simultaneous happenings on the north-west Wales home front show that the area may not have been as quiet as others thought, but it was 'kept quiet'. The population of North Wales was small relative to its size in the years leading up to the outbreak of war. However as hostilities grew a huge influx of people entered the wider area as evacuees, not just children, but government departments, considering it safe despite the proximity to Liverpool and the shipbuilding coast of Lancashire. North Wales was also under the flight path from France to the port of Liverpool, targeted for destruction by Goring and the attack commanded by Hugo Sperrle from Paris.

Many had witnessed the bombing of Liverpool and Birkenhead from the North Wales coast and anticipated that stray bombs may be jettisoned from returning planes. Nevertheless it was one of the relatively safe areas and the influx arrived as planned 'Operation Pied Piper' brought schoolchildren and their teachers to North Wales from Liverpool and had a huge effect and increase on the population. Papers at the National Archives outline estimated numbers of population for the entire country in 1942 for the purposes of planning provisions since there had been no census during 1941.[13]

In theory the North Wales hillsides offered the perfect evacuation spot for families and children from the industrially dense area of Liverpool and its surrounding areas. However in practise the idyllic welsh coastline was far from ideal, being so remote. But this area was not expected to be a target for attack. Geographically, it was quiet, too mountainous for the landing of planes, sparsely populated out of season, and therefore had a plentiful supply of readily available seaside accommodation, and a local population who could work if tourism was displaced. Jill Wallis, in *A Welcome in the Hillside?*, explores in great detail the impact and exactly how welcome, or not, the evacuees were in reality. The expected numbers were never correct and some diversions were made with groups being sent to destinations other than Colwyn Bay. Due to the difficulties with the requisitioning of buildings undertaken by the Ministry of Food the area was already crowded. As the early stages of the war developed and the expected German attack failed to appear many returned home, believing this to be a phoney war and no real danger. On occasions evacuee mothers did not gel with the locals. Language, culture, religion and lack of bars open on 'dry' Sundays contributed, as well as homesickness and perpetuation of false rumours of the poor reception they received.[14] In July 1938 the Anderson Committee had reported the principles of their evacuation policy. The report established that evacuation would not be compulsory although billeting would be; schoolchildren could be moved in school parties in the care of teachers; central government would pay initial costs.

Evacuation was a vital undertaking. The peaceful hillsides were entrusted to shelter more than the Merseyside schoolchildren, and even more than government departments. Protection of the priceless heritage of the nation, art treasures, bomb storage, and also the safety of spies removed from London were valuable contributions. Each aspect had its own impact, some given more recognition than others. The secret relocation of civil servants to the seclusion of coastal seasonal accommodation was a crucial aspect of the process of efficiently feeding the nation.

In addition 'Operation Kindertransport' smuggled two hundred Jewish refugee children out of Nazi Germany into Gwrych Castle close to Colwyn Bay, a building with very basic facilities, unconnected to the mains water or electricity supplies. They remained until 1948 when the State of Israel was created. This has never been common knowledge locally during the war, since then or indeed in the present except to the Abergele community of the day.[15]

On the outbreak of war, firstly the contents of the National Gallery and Hampton Court were stored at six North Wales' destinations including Bangor University, the National Library of Wales in Aberystwyth and Penrhyn Castle (the National Gallery in London was badly damaged by bombing in 1940). Between 23 August and 2 September 1939 6,000 pictures had arrived in the area.[16] But because of risk in raids on Liverpool via Wales eventually it was decided that Manod slate quarry, 1,750 feet above sea level and impervious to air attack with abundant slate protection overhead, would be ideal especially, in view of its remote location, and the operation was completed in 1941. The quarry was not returned to the owners until the 1980s because of the possibility of further wars.[17] GT, a contributor of oral history originally from Gwynedd comments,

> And there was all the storage of pictures in North Wales in the quarries. The impetus for the quarry has gone it will never work again. It must have been thought out for a long time before the war started. They were organised.[18]

Other quarries in Llanberis were used for bomb storage. The Rhydymwyn site near Mold was used to house thousands of mustard gas shells. The eighteenth-century site had been suggested by ICI to Churchill as a possible secret location for chemical weapons.[19] Built approximately five miles away from Colwyn Bay, the 'Mulberry Harbours', floating platforms used in the Normandy landings, were designed by a local man Hugh Iorys Hughes and a prototype assembled on the Conwy Morfa, as a top secret project. A stone installed decades later commemorates 'one of the best kept secrets of the war'.[20] It was a huge project, which was surprisingly kept highly confidential despite the fact that there were thought to be German spies in the area.[21] Even those who assembled it did not realise the purpose. Although the Welsh are reputed to be inquisitive (famously and humorously depicted as so by Dylan Thomas), this was thought to be a good choice of venue, and details of the project would not be 'leaked.'

A local resident remembers what she saw while rock climbing. 'They were the 'landing things'. We could not understand what it was. When we heard about Mulberry Harbour later on then we realised – oh, that is what we saw. It was very secretively done'. [22]

Nationalism had caused some concern, with some Welsh Nationalists not wanting to enlist to fight for England. Language and culture had been to an extent separate from the infiltration of the English over centuries. Wales as a designated reception area with a huge evacuee intake meant that education had to be reorganised in both private and state schools.

Welsh Nationalists objected to a military aerodrome in Penrhos, as a possible target, although it provided employment and an opportunity for local people to contribute. In September 1936, three men, led by Saunders Lewis (who had founded Plaid Cymru in 1925), had set fire to contractors offices and stores at RAF Penrhos, Pwllheli, which put a hundred men out of work. A worse effect was the subsequent publicity at the Old Bailey, which placed Penrhos high on the list of future targets for the *Luftwaffe*. There had been many demonstrations against conscription in the late 1930s. A crowd of about a thousand attended a meeting conducted by a number of Free Church ministers at Pwllheli, the audience adopted, without dissent, a resolution declaring opposition to compulsory military training.[23] An editorial in the *North Wales Weekly News* described a man who wished to have his name struck from the list after obtaining his objectors certificate, and would now rather be in the army than tolerate his wife nagging for him to enlist.[24]

German Foreign Office intelligence had sought to make the most of Celtic Nationalism, using an Irish intermediary to recruit Nationalist spies. In 1941, Lady Rhys Williams said she was 'canvassed as a possible fifth columnist by the wife of the successor of Ribbentrop who sought an admission that Wales was seething with disaffection'. Lady Williams impressed upon her that there was no more loyal a people.[25] Only two Nazi collaborators were identified, but 156 suspects were under MI5 secret surveillance. William Joyce, the infamous Irish propagandist, arrived as a friend and sub-tenant of Philby, father of Kim in 1937. The evacuated variety department of the BBC in Bangor and Llandudno responded to Joyce's broadcasts, (or 'Lord Haw Haw' as he was known) by trying to schedule the most popular entertainment simultaneously.[26]

A file of suspects in the National Archives illustrates the example of P.N.G., a Ministry of Food employee in Colwyn Bay, who also sought employment with the telephone service. His landlady, G.E., had heard him listening to German broadcasts and sketches of the coastline were found in his room. He told her that Britain would not be heavily bombed because Germany did not want the country in ruins after the war. He had registered as a conscientious objector in 1940. His room was searched and correspondence with two Welsh ministers was found, indicating that they were helping him with his case for conscientious objection. It was recommended that in the event of an invasion he should be detained. He did however enlist at a later date.[27]

Other oral evidence from J.L. illustrated the suspicion which made people vigilant.

He [Dad] was in the army, he did not have to go because he had something wrong with his lungs. He was group 2 and he was in the Pioneer Corps and went to London and went on the telephones and through all the prisons and all the people from abroad that they had to segregate – if they were spies ... My mother had two of those people staying in our house N. van de L., and my mother being nosy was a bit suspicious of him and she happened to see him doing the Hitler sign and she reported him to the authorities. I don't know what came of it as I was only a child. He was in the Ministry of Food. He was always on his typewriter and he wore a kilt. I don't think he was a spy, but my mother was suspicious of everything.[28]

Innocuously 'Post Office Box 55, Colwyn Bay' was the coded address for the North Wales Regional Office of MI5.[29] A house demolished in recent years, the Melfort Hotel in Llanerch Road East, Rhos-on-sea, was requisitioned from its owners in order to operate Plan Hegira, in which sanctuary was provided to double-agents brought from London in 1941. If Germany had captured them in the event of an invasion, the information they held would have been too dangerous. The agents and their families would certainly have all been shot by MI5 rather than be allowed to fall into enemy hands. Agents with code names such as Snow, Celery, Dragonfly, Gander, Summer, Careless, Rainbow and Gelatine were removed to North Wales. As well as the Melfort, other hotels in Llandudno, Betws-y-Coed and Tal-y-Cafn were also used.[30]

Coincidentally, another connection with Special Operations exists. An actor who famously played a fictitious spy also has connections with this town. At the end of the war, Timothy Dalton, star of James Bond movies *Living Daylights* and *Licensed to Kill,* was born in Colwyn Bay to an American mother of Italian and Irish descent, and an English father, who was a captain in the Special Operations Executive during the Second World War. He had become an advertising executive at the time of his son's birth.[31]

Contributions to the war in North Wales were diverse, but in the coastal seaside town of Colwyn Bay there was one specific vital function. The successful organisation and administration of the distribution of food affected every person in the country.

# 3: Colwyn Bay and its particular contribution. 'The town was transformed and energised by the war.'[32]

It was expected that this and other reception areas would experience overcrowding to a high degree during the war years. Yet on a positive note some businesses thrived during the war, for example men's hairdressing for soldiers, women's for the female personnel and wives of the Ministry of Food staff. There were said to be some wonderful shops in Colwyn Bay that survived until after the war. Wood's department store, Neville's, Anstiss, Allen's furniture store, some fashionable, high-quality ladies dress shops, Rosie Davies sold furs, which did not require clothing coupons. The Cartmell Hotel, with Pinningtons' bakery below, was known to be a businessman's hotel. It later became Lowe's restaurant, but at the present time is a bar-restaurant called the Prince Madoc.

As in other areas, there was manufacture of munitions, which took place in a local commercial garage. Advertisements could be seen in the local press offering employment to women. Other more exceptional work was the assembly on an intensive scale of jeeps, fifty per day for twenty-two hours per day, for three years

**THE COLWYN BAY FUR CO.**

is a well-known London House of Manufacturing Furriers who, owing to prevailing conditions, have transferred their business to Colwyn Bay and have

**OPENED A SPECIAL DEPARTMENT FOR RE-MODELLING AND RENOVATIONS**

This is an unique opportunity to have your Furs re-modelled by Expert Furriers, keen prices, excellent workmanship, modern styles, satisfaction guaranteed. Speedy service. Your inspection is invited. Estimates given

**25, Princes Drive Colwyn Bay**

*Advert for the Colwyn Bay Fur Company.*
*[NWWN, 21 January 1943]*

continuously. The parts were shipped from America to Liverpool.³³

F.D. worked for Braid's where Jeeps were assembled in 1943, performing general garage duties. By this time he was of age and was awaiting call up papers. His father knew somebody who ran Braid's Garage and they thought it would be good for him to have some experience with the jeeps before joining the RAF. He taught himself to drive.³⁴ He provided a photograph of the jeeps awaiting delivery on Gregory Avenue. Photographs of production of Jeeps with women on the assembly line were also found in the local Records Office in Ruthin. Production lasted for three years, round the clock, using parts shipped to Liverpool from America. F.D. identified the photos of executive staff. Until 1943 Braids had been producing aircraft and engineering products including aircraft engine manifolds and shell cases.³⁵

More exclusively still, a company called Frish & Wins was set up on the top floor of a hardware shop in Princess Drive manufacturing diamond tools for armaments. The diamond industry was of strategic importance during the war effort and not only for manufacturing weapons but as a currency. Equipment such as sawing machinery was consigned from Slamco in New York, but the first delivery was destroyed in a raid on Liverpool. Some tools were produced locally by Dua and Stoeltjes, Belgian refugees. The production would be exported to America as part payment for armaments and other imports under the Lend-lease agreement. Mr Biallostersky, a Dutchman was responsible for the eighteen machine operators. There were also diamond-cutting factories in Bangor with sixty employees where several languages were spoken including Dutch, English, Flemish, French and Welsh.³⁶ Because of the vital contribution to industry and armaments the diamond industry was a reserved occupation. Later it was taken over by J. K. Smit, who also set up another diamond tool factory in Rhos-on-Sea which manufactured stylus and continued operating into the 1950s.³⁷

Contributions at the Frish & Wins factory were diverse. One of the Belgian diamond workers, Eddy De Klerk, had invented some fire fighting equipment and also a machine to convert salt water to fresh, not a completely new idea, but uniquely it was a portable machine that could be used in a lifeboat, and was said to have been given to the Admiralty.³⁸ Another working here as a local teenager during the war when asked if there were any other contributions Colwyn Bay made to the war states pragmatically. 'We were only interested then in going to work and receiving our pay packet.' Reinforcing the view that the industries had contributed significantly to the lives of the young locals.

A benefit of the substantial recruitment into the Home Guard was the release of the army to perform its regular duty. Local men living in North Wales who were unable to enlist in the services for various reasons contributed by enrolling in the Home Guard. There would be branches in every district, comprised of men perhaps too old for conscription. Originally named the Local Defence Volunteers (LDV), they were sometimes called 'Look, Duck and Vanish'. Denbighshire was fortunate in having experienced men who had served in the First World War. Lieutenant-Colonel John R. Williams was an example, and one of the first to join. He had joined the 4th Battalion, Royal Welch Fusiliers when the First World War broke out. Commissioned as a second lieutenant, he served in Rouen, Messines, Passchendaele and Ypres. Others had fought in Flanders and in the Boer War. Williams transferred to the RAF in 1918 and became education officer of the squadron. After the war, he qualified as a solicitor. Other local solicitors also joined the LDV on the outbreak of the Second World War. Major A. I. Edwards-Evans was organiser at Colwyn Bay, Captain Arthur Hughes was responsible for the enrolment in Colwyn Bay, J. D. H. Osborn was in charge at Betws-yn-Rhos and John Williams was lieutenant-colonel in charge of Abergele. His Home Guard regiment's

*Members of the Local Defence Volunteers drilling, 1940. [Bureaucrats in Battledress]*

*Home Guard on parade, about to be inspected by Lord Woolton [Bureaucrats in Battledress]*

motto was *Wastad yn Barod* (Always Ready) and they tried to live up to it.[39] Those too young may have belonged to training organisations such as the Sea Cadets, Army Cadets or the Air Training Corps. There were two ATC units, Colwyn Bay Town (No. 271) and Colwyn Bay County School (No. 1533). Mr F. Davies, a contributor of oral history, was a member of the latter, and has provided photographs of the unit on parade and with many names listed. The CO of the school ATC Squadron was Squadron Leader F. C. Hobbs, the physics master. His officers were Flight Lieutenants E. Evans (geography) and T. O. Griffiths (chemistry).[40] Pupils at a gliding school in the Conwy Valley were taught by pilots who had served in the Royal Flying Corp or Royal Naval Air Service during the First World War.

The Ministry of Food had its own Home Guard company, which became affectionately known as 'Bureaucrats in Battledress'. There were strategically important defence positions – at the headland and the main line railway between Holyhead and Euston. Companies A, B, C, D and E, were set up to cover local geographic areas and when the Ministry of Food came, F company was formed under the command of Major Lawrence, until Lachlan MacLean, OBE, a principal assistant secretary arrived from London in September. Many who arrived in July 1940 had been enrolled in the London guard in preceding months. They were responsible for

Colwyn Bay County School ATC, 1942
Back row: –?–; Brian Menin; Fred Davies; Harod (Gordon) Pearson; Derek Hurlstone; George Wilkinson; Richard Bird (?); Gerald Hughes; –?–; Alan Watt.
Middle row: –?–; Donald Ball; Graham Walker; Tony Moolenar; Ronnie Williams; Gwyn Williams; John Vaughan; Ken Clark; –?–.
Front row: Jack Ashworth; John Hales (?); P.C. Davies/Fred Hughes; Pierre ?; Ken Wheatcroft; Geoff Pritchard; E.J. Evans (Geography); F.C. Hobbs (Commanding Officer; Physics). [Mr F. Davies]

Colwyn Bay County School ATC, 1942
Back row: Alan Watt. Alan Finn; Frank Jordan; Richard Bird (?); Neville Morris; Cecil Owens; Colin Clark; –?–; Dennis Crowley.
Middle row: Ken Clark; –?–; –?–; –?–; –?–; –?–; Cliff Astbury; –?–; –?–; –?–.
Front row: F.C. Hobbs (Commanding Officer; Physics); T.O. Griffiths (Chemistry); derek Hobbs; Jimmy Hobbs; Hesketh Hughes; Bill Davies; –?–; –?–. [Mr F. Davies]

*Colonel Llewellin meets the Auxiliaries.* [Bureaucrats in Battledress]

guarding a section of coastal defences A medical organisation within the Home Guard was authorised in April 1941, and a medical officer was appointed to each battalion with the rank of major. Dr Geoffrey Jones was with B Company and carried out the training.[41]

A special feature of the procession to celebrate the third anniversary of the Ministry unit was a company of Women Home Guards from the Ministry of Food. They received a special ovation from the Colwyn Bay crowd. Miss A. E. French headed the company.[42] It was highly unusual for women to be members of the Home Guard, as researched by Penny Summerville in her book *Contesting Home Defence*.[43] But, as discussed by oral history contributor G.T., and others, there were career women in the workforce of the Ministry, who were also members of the Women's Home Guard. They were not only employees but also the wives who had accompanied the executive civil servants, and some local women had also volunteered. It is evident that Colwyn Bay was a progressive area in this field, clearly due to the influence of the evacuated civil servants.

130 women at the Ministry of Food which had been evacuated to Colwyn Bay in North Wales, formed a unit affiliated to the WHD in September 1942. They were accepted as a 'women's section' wearing the WHD badge, by the Ministry of Food's Home guard. The women were organised in six sections (administration, catering, communications, guides, intelligence and transport.) and took part in night excercises.[44]

# 4: The Ministry of Food
## 'Food town on sea'

The most dramatic change for the town was the relocation of a government department with a vital function. The Food Defence Plans had been formulated in 1936, so by the outbreak of war the Ministry of Food was ready to relocate to Colwyn Bay to start operating in January 1940. The Ministry of Food based its main Headquarters for the whole country there, and Lord Woolton had an office in the Colwyn Bay Hotel. There was a huge impact on the town with 5,000 civil servants and their families relocated. One of the ameliorating effects was the amazing social life which ensued with the coming of outside influences in an era before television had begun to overpower and manipulate as it does in the present. The area was energised and transformed in return for its disruption; all effects are substantiated in interviews. Numerous adverts in the local paper during wartime provide evidence of increased retail and entertainment opportunities. Drama and sport flourished. As early as January 1941 several shows were advertised by the amateur dramatic society.

> The Ministry of Food staff recently demonstrated their talents in the realm of music by giving excellent performances of *The Messiah* last week members of the dramatic society showed their capabilities once more proving that the Ministry is rich in amateur talent. The ambitious programme at the Colwyn Bay Pier Pavilion included four one act plays.[45]

By March 1941 productions of Du Maurier's *Rebecca* and J. B. Priestly's *When we are Married* were staged at the Repertory Theatre, and in April the Music Society gave a concert to a packed audience in the Penrhos assembly hall, the orchestra comprising mainly of Ministry of Food personnel.

> Although the orchestra of thirty eight was augmented by a small number of professional players the majority were members of the Ministry of Food

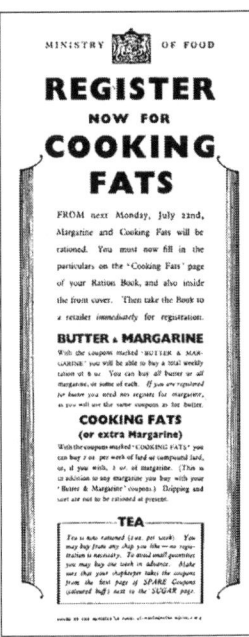
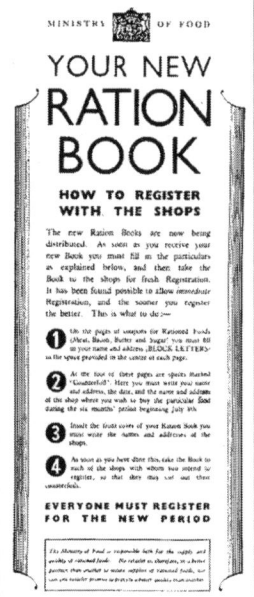
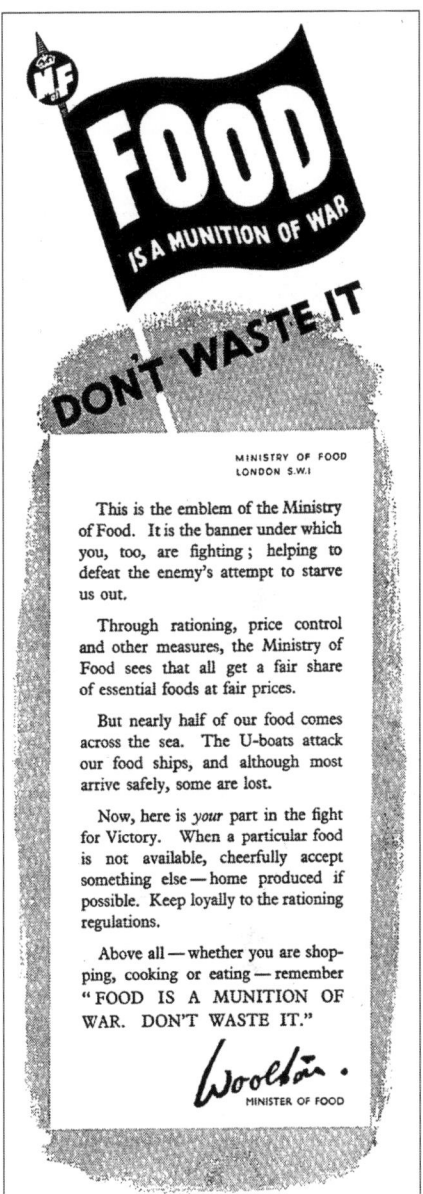

*Adverts illustrating the range of the Ministry of Food's work and the control it exerted over the population.*

which is fortunate to possess this wealth of talent.' The choir consisting entirely of members of the Ministry, numbered nearly one hundred.[46]

The Cricket Club had been founded 1923, the ground and pavilion was opened 10th May 1924. In September 1940 the club engaged in raising money for war charities such as the Mayors' Spitfire Fund. £250 was donated by John Newton. Between 1939 and 1945 special matches were organised by the club and constituted a record contribution from any cricket club. This would have been influenced by the huge influx of newcomers to the town. Monies raised were considerable.[47]

Later oil painting and crafts were exhibited by Ministry of Food staff. An exhibition on Princes Drive, at Selby Towers, was opened by Sir John Bodinar, JP. Items ranged from oil paintings to specimens of illuminated lettering, bookbinding and puppet making. An editorial in the local paper commented

> It is interesting to note the influence of North Wales on the civil servants who have been with us for five years, no hint of nostalgia, no pictures of London, no war pictures, just the hills and the valleys, the farms and castles, groups of boats and birds which all goes to show how much the artists have enjoyed their stay.[48]

Therefore it was evident that both guests and hosts enjoyed a mutually rewarding relationship over more than five years.

| Money raised by Colwyn Bay Cricket Club[49] | |
|---|---|
| 1940 Spitfire fund | £ 675 11 3 |
| 1941 Liverpool and Bootle air raid distress fund | £ 330 0 3 |
| 1942 Mayor of Manchester's Air Raid distress fund | £1296 2 0 |
| 1943 Red Cross prisoners-of-war fund | £3663 12 10 |
| 1944 Red Cross prisoners-of-war fund | £5459 14 11 |
| Local charities | £ 279 16 8 |
| | £11,704 17 8 |

*Lord Woolton inspecting members of the Home Guard. [Bureaucrats in Battledress]*

Lord Woolton, Minister of Food, speaking at Colwyn Bay Food Education week exhibition yesterday warned gamblers in food that he was on their track. 'These people' he said 'must remember that I know something about commercial life, and I am watching some of them. This is the last and final warning that they will get. After all what is the use of making a little extra money illegitimately out of food. It is not going to be of any use to them unless we win this war, and they are not helping us … Why are they allowed to exist? … because they are like the worms of the earth. They slither along and go underground.

Lord Woolton's Final Warning To Gamblers in Food 1941.[50]

The First World War had seen food queues on the high streets of Great Britain. These were a sign of growing centralised control of food distribution but were also evidence of civilian willpower and resilience in support of the soldiers at the front. Just two decades later food supplies were again at risk. Lord Devenport's experience in the 1917 Ministry of food followed by Lord Rhondda in 1918 produced the foundations on which plans were laid to control food production and destitution should a second major conflict erupt.

The Food Control Committee of the First World War gave discretion as to the type of rationing scheme to be adopted and the staple foods to be controlled, including milk, bread, flour, butter, cheese, fish, and potatoes. Later London was brought under a single rationing scheme for meat, butter and margarine which led to its adoption for the whole country which remained in force until 1921 when the first Ministry of Food was closed and the Food Control Committees ceased to function. The Food Control Committees returned during the Second World War to represent consumers in each Local Authority area and to provide efficient local administration, enforcement of the headquarters of the Ministry of Food's orders and handle applications for licences.[51]

The second Ministry of Food was set up under an Order in Council of 8 September 1939, which transferred the functions of holding, using and disposing of stocks and other property held by the Board of Trade's Food (Defence Plans) Department. By another Order of 13 October 1939, the Board of Trade's functions relating to the acquisition, control, storage and prices of certain essential foodstuffs were also transferred. The Minister of Food then became the authority for making, amending and revoking orders relating to the general control of the foodstuffs industry. The first Minister of Food in the Second World War, W. S. Morrison, and Sir Henry French, had been responsible for drawing up the food defence plans and making preliminary purchases before war broke out.[52]

Primary responsibility was to ensure that all sections of the community could obtain necessary food supplies at reasonable prices. In wartime its activities were associated with rationing and state trading. It was responsible for the administration of food subsidies and some of the deficiency payments schemes, and cooperated with other departments concerned in the annual farm price review and the working out of the future basis of guarantees for farmers. Other functions were food defence planning; research into the methods of preparing; marketing and preserving foodstuffs; maintenance and improvement of food standards; advising the public on cooking available foodstuffs and providing for UK representation on various international food bodies.

A document from the Information Division outlines the work of the Ministry

It is the task of the Ministry of Food to provide a national diet which is adequate to safeguard the health of the people and to ensure that the limited food supplies are distributed equitably and at reasonable prices. In order to carry out this task the Ministry has had to establish effective control of the flow of all essential foods from the source to the consumers. It has become the sole purchaser of over ninety percent of the country's food exports, and buys, or controls the sales and prices of practically everything the British farmer produces.[53]

A home production policy was planned in conjunction with the Agricultural departments mindful of the limited space on board vessels for the import of such commodities as animal foodstuffs, and scientific advisors were consulted on the recommendation of what was suitable to grow taking into account the healthy option and also public tastes. Imports were considered carefully and under the lend-lease scheme with America Britain was to receive mainly maize, pork, dairy products canned meat, canned fish, canned beans and dried fruit.

Price control was imposed on nearly all food in consultation with the trade at each stage of distribution. There were subsidies for the very poorest on the main food – flour, bread, potatoes, eggs, meat, and oatmeal, and a national milk scheme covered expectant mothers and children under five. Priority was given to nutrition, particularly for children, and food advice was given to housewives on the 'Kitchen Front' on the wireless in the mornings. A need was recognised to supplement the diet of heavy workers by giving them a special cheese ration so that they could take a packed lunch to work. The British Restaurants were established, 1,068 existing by December 1941. Here a good meal could be obtained very cheaply. They served overall 200,000 meals per day. Famously, rationing was the fairest way to distribute under a points rationing scheme. Also provision was made for emergencies in the form of Queens's Messenger Convoys, which could be sent to any town experiencing heavy bombing, and for food in air raid shelters, and also for those who had lost their homes.[54]

In April 1940, Frederick Marquis (Lord Woolton) was appointed by Chamberlaine for a vital task,[55] replacing the Right Honorable William Morrison as Minister of Food. In his memoirs Lord Woolton stated that the country never realised how close we were to disaster by submarine peril. During the course of two hours one Friday afternoon he received five separate signals from the admiralty that food ships had been sunk on the Atlantic route.⁵⁶ The implementation of the organisation, a vital and complex business was given importance by Lord Woolton, who in an audience with the King explained the need to communicate to the staff of the Ministry how greatly the morale of the country might depend on them. The King promptly visited the London office and followed up with a telegram from the Palace.

> The security of the home front is as vital as that of the Fighting Front and I appreciate to the full the work of the Ministry staff, both in London and throughout the country, in safeguarding the supply and distribution of the people's food.⁵⁷

An *ésprit de corps* was created. There were regional and local food offices the machinery of which had been put in place by Sir Henry French who was head of the administration and accounting officer. Lord Woolton was determined to make the Ministry into 'an easy running machine with civil servants, some permanent some temporary, some trained in government administration, some conducting in peacetime large businesses, some paid, some voluntary ... in short a positive hotch-potch of talent and experience'⁵⁸

The lack of documentation makes the identification of some of the buildings used to house the department within Colwyn Bay problematic. However it is possible through some of the letterheads housed at the National Archives to shed some light on the organisation, for example the Colwyn Bay Hotel, the Metropole and the Pwllychrochan Hotel are all directly referenced. Some records of the work of the Ministry of Food have survived the journey south when the departments returned after the war.⁵⁹ Other functions of buildings were named through the memory and experiences of former employees. As for accommodation of personnel, the North Wales coast had available accommodation ready for immediate occupancy by government staff and offices. These became requisitioned to ensure safe administrative headquarters far away from the Blitz. This was one of the most vital apparatus as a weapon in wartime, the organisation and provision of food for the nation. Neighbouring Llandudno housed the Inland Revenue, another vital function, but one that did not monopolise the town to the same extent. In June 1940, the 5,000 civil servants

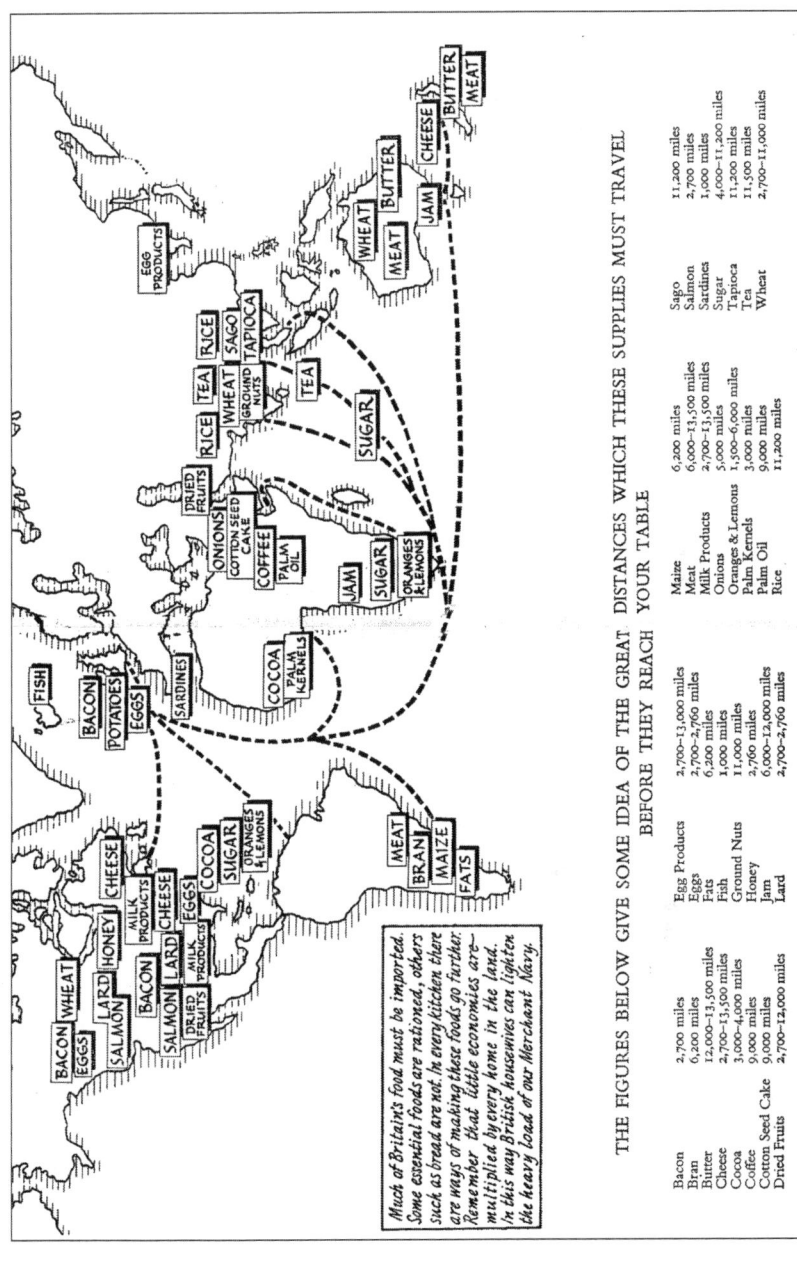

Map of the world showing the distances food travelled by sea. [Memoir of the Earl of Woolton]

*Colwyn Bay Hotel [W. Alister Williams Collection]*

descended in a spectacular influx, stunning the local people. In this small town it would dramatically enlarge the population by 25%.[60] Lord Woolton pragmatically comments in his memoirs, written in 1959, on how little of the Ministry's policy was ever written as memoranda or even minutes. 'This must have been a considerable impediment to the historians ... but businessmen do not write essays on policy'.[61] But, at the time of writing his memoir in 1959, the war was a relatively recent memory and secrecy may have been still instinctive in view of the cold war. A history of the work of the Ministry was commissioned and many documents at the National Archives were marked secret and closed for thirty or more years. Why was the important function of the town so unknown? Was it seemingly unimportant? Did secrecy become a habit? Diaries have been destroyed, lost or even unwritten. But there is oral evidence within the population which it is vital to capture.

Lord Woolton had remained aloof from the social life of Colwyn Bay, staying at a hotel in Llandudno Junction and maintaining an office in Whitehall as well as in the Colwyn Bay Hotel. He mentions the town only once in his memoir, in relation to a train journey. However, as a businessman, he got the job done.

A letter to the editor of the *North Wales Weekly News* on 10 April 1941, from the librarian of the National Library of Wales appealed to the public to preserve any material relating to Wales and the war.[62] Even diaries were being recycled, and valuable information being lost. An article in February 1943 appeals for paper saving in an imaginative way, and informs how much paper, although in short supply, it was necessary to use.

> The Ministry uses over 4000 tons of paper every year and one and a half million envelopes … If each employee saves one quarto sheet of paper per working day it will save 35 tons a year and these placed end to end would stretch from Rhos pier to the Dingle.[63]

Colwyn Bay's contribution is rarely mentioned. Even the obituary of John Raeburn, a statistician and head of the Agricultural Plans branch, the senior figure responsible for the hugely successful 'Dig for Victory' campaigns, published in the *Telegraph* and the *Times* on 22 July 2006, the glowing tributes do not mention the town where his valuable work took place, just a vague reference to 'North Wales'. Raeburn was one of the influx who married a local woman. [64]

Some documents still in existance have given insight into the machinations of the steps carried out to requisition buildings to house the Ministry once the decision to evacuate from Whitehall had been made.

> An agent will be instructed to requisition certain buildings. He will serve the formal notice of requisition, obtain vacant posses-

*Digging for Victory, and now we are recommended to do it again). Demobbed from the RAF after the war, two insurance agents, Bob Roberts and Tom Roberts, near Greenfield Road. [Author's collection]*

sion, take a schedule of condition of the building and make an inventory of its contents. It will be essential that the agent shall work at the highest speed in order that the premises shall be available for government use at the earliest possible moment.[65]

A government paper, marked 'Secret' and entitled 'Agents' Emergency Work Outline Procedure' summarizes how to obtain vacant possession.

> The occupier must be informed that all persons in the building except staff, are to vacate in six hours, taking with them all their personal belongings. Actual possession will not be taken until the visitors, etc have vacated the premises, or at the expiration of six hours.
> The occupier (or, in the case of an hotel, the Manager) may remove all perishable food and other valuables, articles, etc which he wishes providing this is done within the space of a few hours.
> N.B. Before the inventory and schedule of condition is commenced the manager shall be requested to see that his staff, before they leave, and under his supervision, remove all wines, spirits, imperishable food, linen, silver, crockery, valuables, etc., into a room for temporary storage. This room must be locked and sealed in the presence of the manager. (Rooms suitable for this purpose, e.g. pantries, linen rooms, cupboards, etc., must be selected on account of dryness, etc., but as far as possible, rooms suitable for office accommodation shall not be used) .
> As soon as this has been done the staff must vacate the building, and if discharged by the management can seek re-employment by HM Office of Works, in accordance with the notice affixed in the entrance hall.[66]

Evidence of oral history contributor Albert Rigby (a teenage clerk in the information bureau) in chapter 6 underpins the preliminary processes of requisitioning when two senior officials visited in the spring of 1940.[67] Papers, some marked 'Secret', give evidence of the actions of the Ministry of Food when the decision was made to relocate. On 4 July 1940, a letter from the Dominions Office, Downing Street to the Secretaries of the High Commission for Canada; Commonwealth of Australia; High Commissioner of New Zealand; High Commissioner for the Union of South Africa; High Commissioner for Eire and High Commissioner for Southern Rhodesia, officially notified that the headquarters of the administration of the Ministry of Food had been evacuated to Colwyn Bay.

*Metropole Hotel, Penrhyn Road. [Francis Frith Collection, 46270]*

I am directed by Viscount Caldecote to request you to inform the High Commissioner that It was recently decided that the administrative staff of the Ministry of Food should be evacuated from London to the provinces. This evacuation has now been carried out, The headquarters of the Ministry of Food are now at Colwyn Bay, Denbigh[shire] North Wales, and communications intended for the Ministry (other than the fresh fruit and vegetables branch) should in future be sent to that address. The address of the Fresh Fruit and Vegetables branch is St John's College Oxford.

This letter was signed by P. G. Clutterbuck.[68]

A letter of 11 July 1940 from Johnston of the Burma Office, Whitehall, to Hutton, Ministry of Food, discusses liaison arrangements.

I am afraid that I find some difficulty in replying to your letter on the 5th of July regarding the liaison between our two departments. My difficulty arises partly from the fact that we have no information as to what has happened to the Ministry of Food We do not know the function of that part which has remained in London, what divisions are at Colwyn Bay or what are their functions, nor do we know where the other divisions are or what they do.[69]

He requested a paper drawn up showing the layout of the Ministry of Food, and to know what work was being undertaken.[70] If officials in the department did not know to where it had relocated then the enemy would never find it! Although it would seem apparent at first that the Ministry had vanished, and the right hand seemed not to know what the left hand was doing, today we marvel at the efficiency and the way administrators coped to produce the right results in view of the difficult conditions in which they worked, knowing that miscommunications are today still often inevitable even with the advantages of advanced technology of the present.

Another communication from Van Zwanenberg at the Hotel Metropole, Colwyn Bay, to a Mr Wheeldon, dated 26 November 1940, concerns priority phone calls and their degree of urgency.

> After receipt of your circular about Priority and Trunk telephone calls we had a long talk in this division as to how we could most fairly operate to avoid asking for priority when it was not necessary ... I do not think I have asked for half a dozen telephone calls since the Ministry has been here. I have had to ask for it [priority] on two occasions in the last three or four days and this morning after waiting two hours I have just been informed that there are still nineteen priority calls ahead of me.

Van Zwanenberg wanted to purchase three-and-a-half-million cases of oranges from Spain and was concerned that the difficulties would compromise diplomatic relations. Present-day administrators could not fail to applaud the success of arrangements covering vital work under extreme adversity, with the removal of the department hundreds of miles away, few phone lines and limited supplies of paper.[71]

If enemy action had severed telephone links, contingency plans were in place in the form of carrier pigeons, which would have dispatched any necessary dramatic revisions in rationing to strategic centres. The pigeon loft apparently remained in place behind the former [now demolished] Colwyn Bay Hotel until 1975. To protect these pigeons from being devoured by a predator, along with their messages, the Home Guard had shot and eliminated the rare peregrine falcons on the Great Orme.[72]

A letter to Mr Maud from Lord Woolton conveyed his appreciation of the work of his employees and regretting that the serious paper shortage prevented him from thanking each one personally.

It must be some reward to know that Britain is well, and for the part you have played in achieving this, and I am personally and deeply conscious of all the help that you have given me in doing my work.[73]

Lord Woolton's letter was sent on 26 December 1941, with good wishes for Christmas, and stamped 'Received' at Maud's office on 14 January 1942. Of the members of the Ministry staff interviewed in 2007, none of them remembered having received this message.[74]

Also from Woolton to Sir Quintin Hill on 14 August 1940 was sent 'to all on return' a request for information, for half a dozen articles on the work of the division, to pass on to the public as an alternative to the press finding

```
                         copy         MINISTRY OF FOOD,
                                        Portman Court,
                                         LONDON, W.1.
                                       26th December 1941

Dear Maud,
   I should have liked to send to every member of the
staff of the Ministry a letter of appreciation of the
work that they have done during this last year, but in
view of the paper shortage I felt it was not right to
do this. I hope therefore, that you will convey the
contents of this letter to all the members of your
staff.
   I am very conscious of the great efforts that have
been made by you all during the year. It must be some
reward to know that Britain is well, and for the part
that you have played in achieving this, and I personally
am deeply conscious of all the help that you have given
me in doing my work.
   With all good wishes for Christmas and the New Year,
believe me to be,
                    Yours sincerely,
                        (sgd.) Woolton.
J. P. R.Maud Esq.,
General Department.
Received 14 January 1942
```

*Copy letter from Lord Woolton [National Archives, MAF 83/945]*

out about bad news, since the story of failure is always better news value than the story of commonplace success.

It seems a report was commissioned on 17 August 1940. Howard Marshall became the first Director of Public Relations at the Ministry of Food from 1940 to 1943, then Director of War Reporting and a war correspondent. He also coached Lord Woolton in his broadcasting technique, and even how to write the script.[76] Marshall was later to famously broadcast from a Normandy beach immediately after the D-Day landings. He wrote to a Mr Vincent that a series of twelve articles should be prepared at the request of the Minister. This was to be undertaken by Beverly Nichols for a fee of twenty guineas an article – less than his usual journalistic remuneration. Nichols said the task had defeated him and he passed the 15,000 words to a man named Beckles who was to continue. Through many memos it seems that Beckles was kept waiting without information and described his treatment as being 'like a naughty schoolboy outside the headmaster's office for more than five days.' A minute sheet of 8 August 1941 stated that Beckles had been paid £21 for each of three articles: *Food town on Sea, The Butcher* and *The Dairy*. Robert Westerby, an author, had written a note to Howard Marshall on 6 June 1942. 'From what I can remember of this book I don't see that it will be very much 'out of date'. It would have made a very good broadcast series if it had been handled at the right time. He was not anxious to be involved – 'Getting into this seems to me very much like getting into a ring with twelve blindfold men, need I do that?'[77]

Other correspondence of 2 January 1942 depicts sketches of a fishmonger and a baker, which had been approved, but not the 'advice centre'. The comment was 'not flattering to the Ministry of Food, as the girl at the desk should be lovely, womanly, Marlene-ish and young. Aren't all Ministry of Food advice centre staff charmers?'

The articles were turned into 'wireless fodder'. The general lines were described as 'The Battle for Food' and should contain information about convoys, the present difficulties as compared with the last war and the varied activities of Ministry of Food including salvage, enforcement and emergency feeding. A detailed schedule of functions and persons to consult ensued for guidance. Interesting stories were suggested such as the salvage of foodstuffs damaged by enemy action e.g. the arrangements for using the carcases of beasts killed in air raids, the treatment and use of sea-damaged cereals; the readiness of people to dispense with luxury and unnecessary articles.⁷⁸

At the Imperial War Museum, Albert Rigby's papers describe the experience of living through the war in the town and his employment as a local man at the Ministry.⁷⁹ A. Ebert, MBE, had a senior position as a senior trade officer with milk products and returned to either Bryanston Square or Stanmore after the war, according to the list compiled by Rigby. Ebert had been one of the civil servants evacuated out of London. His file contains many letters from former local staff who had worked as clerks before being conscripted and had written informatively and with affection to their employer from their new posts with the theme of returning to 'civvy street' after demobilisation. He explains the nature of his work in a reserved occupation coordinating the distribution of butter and cheese and is confident that his expertise was more useful in his own post than if he were to relocate as a soldier. 'Everything went smoothly where I had influence'.⁸⁰

# 5: Social, cultural and economic effects of the influx

Changes and influences on the lives of the locals – particularly women.

> We women are involved in this war as much as the menfolk. There will be greater trials during the next few months but the sacrifices we may be called upon to make will be worthwhile for the best things in life come from home and family life.     March 1941.[81]

> 1,000 women wanted to build aircraft. Married women this is your chance to make famous British fighter and bomber planes. Full or part time employment ... Many women with household responsibilities are now employed.     January 1943[82]

Many areas in Britain had similar evacuee experiences to that of North Wales. The mixing of social classes and differing attitudes to life brought conflict and at times harmony. However the influence of the civil servants from the Ministry made Colwyn Bay's experience unique. The arrival of the civil servants hugely disrupted the town by overcrowding, and eliminated the town's usual main income, which was tourism. The effect would be irreversible. The social mixing, in the case of the evacuees, highlighted a poverty that the middle classes may not have previously encountered. Sir William Beveridge was under-secretary at the Ministry of Labour (1940) and was chairman of the Social Service Inquiry (1941–2) He produced *Social Insurance and Allied Services*, a report prepared for government which proposed a social system 'from the cradle to the grave' for British citizens. This became known as the 'Beveridge Report' and became the blueprint for the welfare-state legislation of 1944–8.[83] Two extremes were witnessed in Colwyn Bay. At one end of the scale the evacuees exposed extreme poverty and at the other the civil servants brought a degree of sophistication.

The social fabric of the North Wales town was disrupted by the war.

Local men of optimum age, who were fit, enlisted. However, those local youths who were awaiting call up papers, were glad to find employment. This new employment was better paid than a catering job or any other connected with tourism. In fact the requisitioning of all the hotels had changed the nature of tourism in this town even before the trend in which it became popular to go abroad in the 1950s.

The local women were involved in housing 'guinea pigs', (as the civil servants were affectionately known because they paid one guinea a week,) or soldiers back from Dunkirk, evacuee children, or worked in munitions at the shell plant. They also applied for administrative work. As discussed by oral-history contributor G.T., and others, there were 'career women' in the incoming workforce of the Ministry. There were also the wives who had accompanied the executive civil servants. These women together with some local women had volunteered to join the Home Guard. It is evident that Colwyn Bay was a progressive area regarding women in the Home Guard and perhaps due to the influence of the incoming civil servants. A procession to celebrate the third anniversary of the Battalion was held and a special feature was a company of women Home Guards from the Ministry of Food. They received a special ovation from the Colwyn Bay crowd. Miss A. E. French headed the company.[84] Women's involvement

*Colonel Barton, CBE, MC, takes the salute as the Auxiliaries march past in a Wings for Victory parade. [Bureaucrats in Battledress]*

*Auxiliaries being inspected by Controller Chitty [Bureaucrats in Battledress]*

had been 'hidden' or made invisible. Although Edith Summerskill fought for their inclusion, it was highly unusual for women to be members of the Home Guard.[85]

In wartime, women had to work somewhere, whether in a caring or domestic role or they would otherwise move into work they would not otherwise have contemplated before wartime, for example production lines. Some daughters would not be permitted by their fathers to join the Women's Air Force like G.R. and G.T. G.R.'s sister was a typist for the Ministry, another sister was a printer and then she went to work at the Estate Agents. Those who ran boarding houses providing accommodation for civil servants, soldiers, American army nurses and G.I.'s remained unaccredited. One such guesthouse housed the Australian crew of a Lancaster bomber who made frequent visits following their raids on Germany. The Americans were amazed to see how healthy the British were on their meagre rations, how the landladies managed, and would not accept any food.

It was evident by numerous oral testimonies that many of the employees at the Ministry of Food were women. Also photographs at Braid's Garage illustrate women working on munitions and in the assembly of jeeps, but in the entire parish records of marriages at two churches 1939–45, no bride

*Jeep assembly line at Braid's, Colwyn Bay. [Stuart Bale Collection via DRO DD/DM/1176/1]*

gave any occupation. Women also contributed significantly to welfare within organisations such as the Women's Voluntary Service, and in housing evacuees but rarely disclosed an occupation on their marriage certificate.

Opportunities for further research lie in the marriage records, which illustrate the constant flux of population verified and experienced by the witnesses. For an accurate result every church and chapel and civil ceremony would have to be accounted for, including Welsh chapels and also civil ceremonies, and to compare these with previous and subsequent years. As no bride gave an occupation, that of her father was entered on the database. There is much evidence of intermarriage and social mobility through demographic changes throughout the war.

Records chosen for investigation were from the two churches most central to the town, i.e. the Parish Church of St Paul, and the nearby St

*Women working with munitions at Braid's, Colwyn Bay. [Stuart Bale Collection via DRO DD/DM/1176/1]*

John's Methodist Church. All records from two churches were printed from microfilm before being transferred to a database. In total 215 marriage records of 430 individuals were interrogated.[86] While none of the brides disclosed any occupation it is proved through interview with G.R., and G.T. and others, that wives worked at the Ministry of Food.

Of the 215 grooms' addresses on the marriage certificates, 87 separate locations were disclosed and 41 of them were military men who came from an area far afield, substantiating the theory of H.P. who said that men in the services found brides in areas where they were posted. Four locations were coded.

1. The Town Centre.
2. Very local or from the conurbation areas including Llandrillo, Llandudno, Tan Lan, Penrhyn Bay and Penmaenrhos.
3. Outlying areas, including any other parts of Wales, including South Wales.
4. From a great distance – England or Scotland and abroad.[87]

*Completed jeeps parked near Braid's Garage [F. Davies]*

It was seen that seventy-two women married men from Area 4, but only sixteen local men married women from outside the area. Some of these men may have been billeted locally in army headquarters. Since the women did not disclose their occupation it is difficult to speculate why they chose to travel to Colwyn Bay to marry unless it was to join fiancés transferred there. There were over seventy couples from similar addresses or neighbourhoods, or perhaps some met through their father's occupation, for instance one daughter of a minister of religion married a clerk in holy orders.

When the filter is applied to Colwyn it is seen that 285 of the 430 of the total individuals resided there. To simplify, at least one of the couple has to be a resident to be able to marry in the local church. Few had been married before, there were no divorcees of either sex recorded and few were widowed. Some may have been older couples and these would write their age as 'Full'. Some lived at the same address, but we would assume one would be a lodger and they would probably not be a common law couple. One of these was the youngest man of twenty.

**Count of Marriages at St Paul's and St John's churches during the Second World War.**

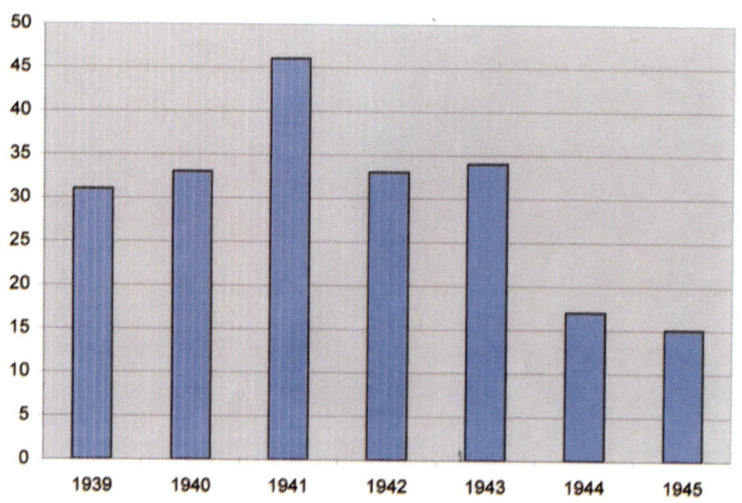

There were 42 military personnel from Area 4 who gave their address as 'Non-local', including members of the armed and supporting services, e.g. wireless operator and inspector, from as far afield as the USA or Canada, and thirty-two civilian occupations were recorded for men from an outside area. The military were further categorised as Air, Sea, Army (with 'S' for unspecified soldier and 'U' for unclassified) and a pie chart indicates the numbers. Only five of the civilian grooms had the occupation of civil servant, but some of the fathers of the brides were civil servants. Social mobility could only be found by using a father's occupation since although we know all women had to work at something, it was not customary for brides to disclose it, which is a serious disadvantage to the research. There was only one bride found who wrote on her marriage certificate that she worked for the Ministry of Food and this was in fact after the war had ended. Another bride interviewed outside of the study, and not from either of the churches had disclosed her army number on her marriage certificate.[88]

The average age of all was twenty-seven. Results were assessed separately for youngest and oldest, the youngest woman being eighteen and the youngest man twenty. The oldest man was 66 and the oldest woman was 58 (except that some wrote only 'Full' age.) Of those aged over 30, there were 40 women and 62 men. Only sixteen women married when

*Toc H canteen ladies at Douglas Road. [A. Davies]*

under the age of twenty-one, which was the age of majority at the time. They would have had to obtain parental consent from their father. The record showed that they generally had their parents as witnesses. Only one man under twenty-one, Joseph W. King, married, to a woman aged twenty, from the same address.

One of the biggest problems is that women did not disclose their occupations at all – so it is impossible to say why they had moved out of their area to marry. There is evidence that there were female employees at the Ministry of Food who had relocated from other areas. We must remember also that in some cases, for example teachers, women often were obliged to resign from their employment when they married.

**Classification of occupations of grooms during the war at St Paul's and St John's.**

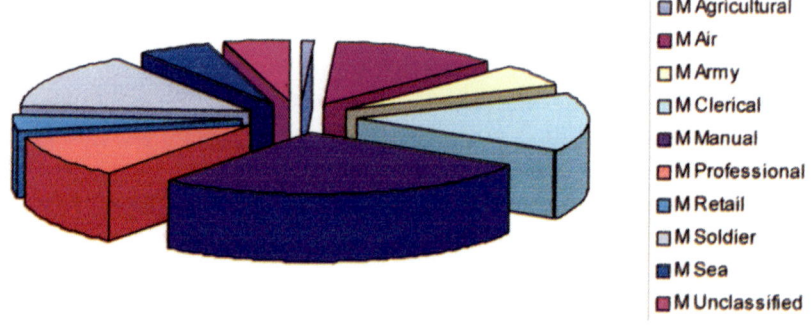

The evidence shows a certain amount of intermarriage through demographic change and many contributors can quote examples. A.W. knows of local families who relocated through their wartime civil service careers, one emigrated to America through her marriage. Her husband became an attorney – possibly a senator. Sir Bertram Chrimes, who had been head of Cooper's of Liverpool, became organiser of Wartime Meals and all the British Restaurants over the country. His daughter became a doctor and had a practice with her husband locally.[89] There were many wartime romances and local women married soldiers they met at the Pier dances. Names were mentioned. This restructuring had a huge impact and is worthy of much further research. HP thinks there were more local men marrying women local to their training ground in all parts of the country.

Flux of population was constant with sudden orders to move into another area all over the country. 'If it hadn't been for the war I would not have married my wife'.⁹⁰ But G.T. relates the story of a Gwynedd family, where they were very 'dyed-in –the-wool Welsh' where one lady, whose daughter married an English airman, never went out afterwards as she was so ashamed that her daughter had married an Englishman.

> There was far too much interbreeding at that time everybody would be a cousin of somebody you knew but now there was new blood. Girls left and went to live in New Zealand and all over the place, and I think it has come back to be a bit more insular again.⁹¹

H.F. says the Townswomen's Guild was for merchants of the town, they were very active and the churches had knitting circles and each church had an afternoon when they did knitting using khaki and the colours of the troops. The women should be gainfully employed, that was the terminology, even if it was looking after evacuees. J.L.'s mother was cashier in the British Restaurant, the cinema and also at the swimming pool. D.R. agreed that, before the war, women could get jobs in a shop or something, but office jobs changed their lives. So the townspeople contributed to the war effort and the Ministry of Food in return contributed greatly to the lives of women. G.T. commented on these women who dressed up to go to work at 8.30am.

> Our mothers found it very difficult to come to terms with. They[working wives] could not have had very clean houses, when did they do their housework, make their beds and scrub the kitchen? It was a totally different way of living. Everything about them was an eye opener for us and so were we for them – there were English inner city children who did not believe that milk came from cows and they could not believe that in a family there was no fighting, no one was throwing plates! It was a new world opening for us. We must have lived a very quiet sort of life before the war. It was good for us I suppose. There was this big influence of these people coming in from Liverpool. The only thing we knew was that you went there to shop, nothing about the type of people who lived there, and then of course there were Londoners which was a new culture altogether, because we had our mothers at home who had never gone out to work, who stayed home and cooked and cleaned and washed and wore an apron and were very homely and here you had women who wore lipstick and had their hair done before

they went out to work in the morning as civil servants. It was either work or go into the army for women between sixteen and fifty five, my mother was very worried and she became ill and had epileptic attacks. When I married there was no question of me staying on at work. My husband was a postman on shifts. During the war all women had to be employed doing something and this is something that had never happened before. There had to be jobs for the men coming back. If there had been a chance of promotion in the office I was in, a man would have had it, but there were only old men who would not have been called up. The general thing was that women did not have promotions, they went to work did a job and came home and did not go into the pension scheme. The hours were long, a 48-hour week. Half past 8 until 6 o'clock with an hour off for lunch, Saturday morning as well, which after the war did not stop immediately. [92]

All over the world, women's lives were changed irreversibly by the war. It is fascinating to hear from each one who experienced the war years.

## 6: Oral history – reflections. Evidence of the former population

I was determined to collect precious stories from as many contributors as I could find and my tenacity in seeking contributors and arranging meetings brought more rewards than I had ever imagined. I was passionate about the topics and certain that it was a beneficial experience for the contributors too. I was delighted to be told by an observer that I had extended one lady's life by five years by encouraging her reminiscence. I was aiming to collect testimony, observations and interpretations of the wartime population on their reflections on the influx of population, both the Ministry staff and others, evacuees from northern cities Liverpool and Manchester, the soldiers drafted here on training exercises, including the Americans and the effect changes had on education, religion, marriages and womens' position in society.

All contributors agreed that the arrival of the department of the Ministry of Food provided many work opportunities and prospects for local people and in many cases led to their achieving permanent positions as established civil servants in London and Guildford. A. Rigby represented the UK in the EEC in Brussels, was a member of the Balance of Payments Forecasting Committee and the World Economic Prospects Committee for thirteen years, a career which stemmed from his early involvement with the Ministry of Food in Colwyn Bay.[93]

The civil servants paid a guinea a week for accommodation and were affectionately (or otherwise) known as 'Guinea Pigs'. Some families would prefer to accommodate them rather than Liverpool children as landladies were shocked by the small recompense for the latter's accommodation.

When asked if all integrated well it was apparent from several interviews that the local people were completely unprepared for the degree of poverty witnessed with regard to those evacuee children from Scotland Road, Liverpool. There had also been concern over clothing supplies. This confirms the work of Jill Wallis.[94] There were many anecdotes related in

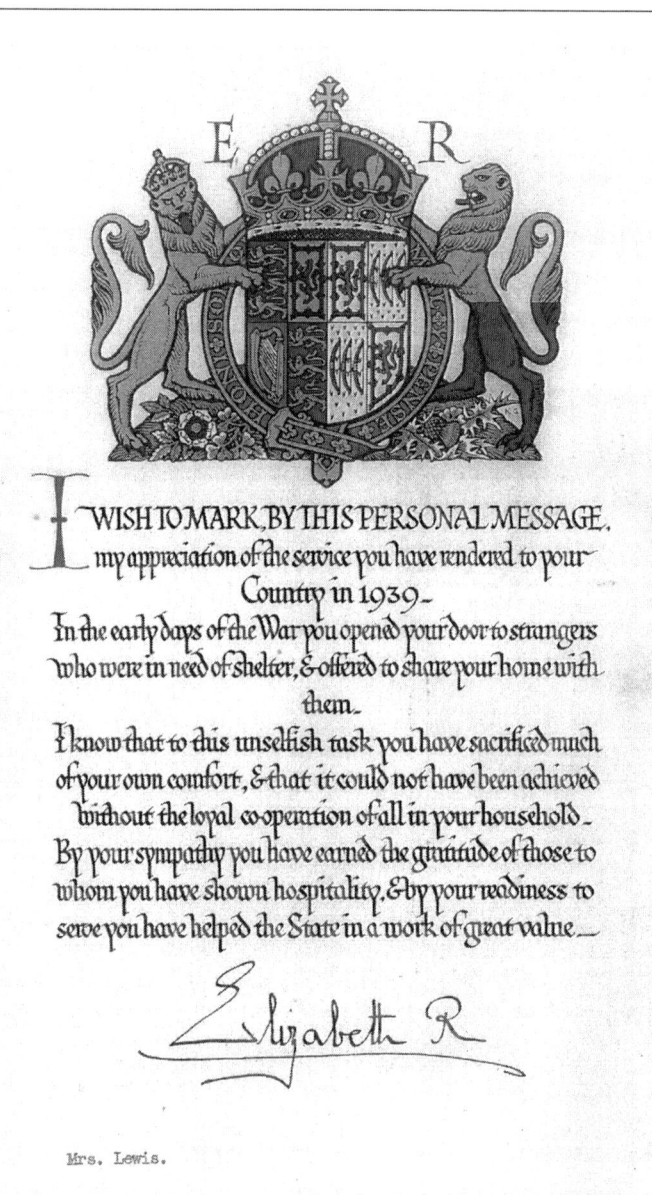

Certificate of thanks to Mrs Lewis for hosting evacuees. [Mrs Diana Roberts]

the interviews regarding bathing, sleeping arrangements, habits, and fleas. It was said to be a revelation for the locals to discover how other people lived, and they were shocked by the degree of difference.[95] This was apparently happening in all parts of the country where city folk were relocated and observations gave rise to the Beveridge Report since, typically, the classes mixed all over Britain for the first time. Here in Colwyn Bay we had the middle-class Londoners, the extreme poverty from Liverpool, and the mixed local population of English and Welsh.

I visited J.L. in the local hospital to interview her. She highlights the antipathy between the Welsh and English, since the English had been arriving for centuries, but not on such a scale.

> I think the Welsh seemed subservient to the English. It opened eyes. We thought we were poor then we saw these coming from the streets of Liverpool, the nuns came to make sure they were alright and my mother said 'Now you are alright, but we are not Catholics'. They wrote home that we were cruel to them because they were not used to discipline, but we had a good home life, and my red shoes disappeared. My father wrote. But she had been to confession so that was alright then![96]

The oral evidence underpins newspaper reports in the *North Wales Weekly News* on 14 March 1940, a survey entitled 'Our Wartime Guests – Opportunity or Menace' concluded that the evacuation scheme had 'not entirely broken down'.[97] The result was expected to modify the national character and destroy the rich individuality of the nation.[98] There was an appeal by the Mayor to all householders in the borough on 27 June 1940 for households to take in civil servants as lodgers, as many as they could, so that compulsory billeting should not arise.[99] Some would take Ministry staff or private evacuees in order to fill up their houses, as they would otherwise have been compelled to take in Merseyside evacuees. When they came, the evacuees had never seen the sea before –

> … they used to go to St Joseph's [Catholic] church poor little things with their gas masks, broken biscuits and their tin of corned beef. John said to my mother ' You never sit on the doorstep Mrs Jones like my mother' – because of course in Liverpool that's what they did'.[100]

One family went as far as selling up to a college who needed a larger building. The Wireless College trained extra students as telegraph operators during the war. The Southampton branch was evacuated to Colwyn Bay during the war. Approximately 600–700 students were trained during the war years.[101]

P.B. speaks of the acute shortage of housing, which lasted until after the war, this can be seen in many issues of the *North Wales Weekly News*. She was an evacuee from the Wirral who after the war remained in Colwyn Bay for the rest of her life. Her family's business had been destroyed in the bombing. The neighbour's house was bombed and all utilities were shut off, and, as she was just out of hospital, she was deemed unfit to join the Wrens. At 28, she had never worked. From her clerical work she went on to become a civil servant with Ministry of Food and, as a single woman, made it her lifelong career.

> I went to the Labour Exchange and the young lady said 'Which service will you go into?' And I had to tell her that I had been in hospital and I could not join up. I was having an appendix operation during the twelve consecutive nights that Liverpool was bombed. I had wanted to go into the Wrens but they would not take you if you had been in hospital for the simple reason that they weren't prepared to pay you a pension for the rest of your life.
>
> So they sent me to the munitions factory in Llandudno Junction and I wasn't very well received because I had never been to work until the war came. They said 'I'm sorry you are no use to us. You will not be able to cope with twelve hours standing. We want people who have been in shops or hotels and are used to being on their feet.' So I went back to the employment exchange and there was a big notice on the counter to say 'Women urgently wanted to work at Braid's' [garage]. It was taken over during the war for munitions. The gentleman there said he had a proposition to make me, he would be prepared to take me into the office as a wages clerk, but there were doubts. The manager at Braids said 'I've nothing against you but I don't think you should do it. The foreman was asked and he came in and said in front of me ' She's no use to us'… in front of me!
>
> I went back to the Labour Exchange and the lady there said 'You've been turned down twice in the same day!' Yes it's gone against the grain that I was a lady of leisure before. As soon as the Ministry of Food moved to Colwyn Bay I asked if I could go to the civil service. I went the recruiting office in Marine Road, corner of Princes Drive and I was taken straight away. They liked to place people as near as possible to their home and there wasn't a job for me at first at the Queen's Hotel. Of course every hotel was

taken over by the Ministry of Food. In a few days I got a note to say that there was a vacancy. I went to the department called Wartime Meals in a section called Queens Messenger Convoys. And from this came the growth of the Womens' Royal Voluntary Service'. What a good idea it was for war and peacetime. It started as the WVS, then it was the WRVS, and I worked for them for 25 years. A lady started it [Lady Reading] with a group of influential friends and it grew so it spread all over the country. We had clothing sections you see, I did a lot of knitting before I found work, we used to sit and knit all morning before. I was a member after the war too for many years until 1982.[102]

Contributors remember that there was a baseball match between American nurses and Ministry of Food personnel, H.F. says:

Yes they travelled by sea to Liverpool and they came here to get their land legs. They had been very seasick on the journey over. They put up square tents on Rydal playing fields to practice.' AW says the corps of US nurses were billeted in houses near to Rydal school 'They set up something called the PX where they could get all the American sweets and nylons. They were not thin, they were motherly. They mixed to a certain extent, were very friendly, they wanted to give us children sweets to get to know us. Some would say 'I am a cowboy from Texas I'll tell you all about it'.[103]

Locals had heard of Texans through the cinema and there were already several in the town. P.B. agreed with G.R.'s comment that it was 'the US personnel who encouraged smoking in the area. Oh yes, definitely, that's how you started.' D.B. says. 'The American soldiers arrived and were received with apprehension. The locals had never seen black people before. They used to go to dances at the YMCA.' (There would have been other ethnicities in Liverpool, but not everyone travelled as far afield in those days) but P.R. maintains that they were mainly stationed in Prestatyn a few miles down the coast, and the consensus was that the locals disapproved of their segregation.' A.R. says the Americans were amazed to see how the landladies managed, and would not accept any food. His mother-in-law was a landlady who had an American GI staying at her house. Strangely, he signed the visitors' book and, under nationality, wrote 'German'.[104]

## Schools and the effect on education during war

Dr Wainwright was born in Old Colwyn. He attended Rydal School and, with the imminent arrival of the Ministry of Food, was one of the boys chosen to help with the removal of some of the furniture when the boys were evacuated to Oakwood Park in the Conwy valley. He was a GP in Colwyn Bay from 1957 until 1985, then retired to Deganwy. He has always been interested in the local history of the area and, blessed with a pictorial memory, has recollections which go back to about 1927. He recalls his memory of wartime.

> After the declaration of war by Chamberlain, the Air Raid Sirens sounded almost straight away, and we all thought the bombers were on the way, but it turned out to be a false alarm, and then there was a phoney war when nothing much happened for a while. During this time we heard that the Ministry of Food were coming to Colwyn Bay and requisitioning Penrhos and Rydal and we had been told that Oakwood Park up the Sychnant Pass had been acquired by Rydal. It had been a five Star Hotel with an eighteen hole Golf Course as part of the grounds. It was suggested that some of the local Rydal boys might like to help with the move so some of us went up there to carry out hotel furniture and carry in desks, etc. It was all quite amazing that there was a relatively smooth transition, and with the general ethos of Rydal at the time which was to be helpful to others and everyone pitched in, the joiners making laboratories out of some of the out buildings, the chaplain scrubbing the kitchen floors the state of which had reduced the school housekeeper to tears, and everyone doing what they could to ensure the school could start up at the beginning of the winter term.
>
> Sadly all my contemporaries who lived locally at the beginning of the war are no longer with us, or they have moved to other parts of the UK where they are frail themselves or looking after relatives who are even more so. There is one friend who was at Penrhos but she was evacuated to Chatsworth when the Ministry of Food requisitioned their building in Colwyn Bay.[105]

The girls of Penrhos College were invited to spend the war in Chatsworth House as the guests of the Duke of Devonshire.[106] Ironically many of the sons of those working in the requisitioned buildings were enrolled as pupils at the temporary Rydal site. Many of the Ministry employees had school-age children who would have to go to the local schools.

There was naturally widespread disruption affecting education when the evacuees arrived en masse. Some required Catholic schools and there was only one, St Joseph's primary school. Some Liverpool teachers came with the pupils and one in particular was more glamorous than any other, with long hair like Veronica Lake, nail varnish and lipstick. 'We all wanted to be like Miss Walsh,' said G.T. Apparently she was influential in other ways, introducing new subjects such as drama, speech training and choral speaking.[107] Schools moved around to various sites, private schools moving out to accommodate the Ministry of Food and otherse.g. Blackburn House, moving to Colwyn Bay for the safety of the pupils. The schools were so full that shift systems were in operation.[108] A.W. confirms the shortage of teachers and some upset that was caused initially. The Liverpool children generally went to the Central School where they did not have a two-tier shift system.[109]

> They hired the Girl Guide Hall and had 2 or 3 classes in there to accommodate those from Liverpool as well, how those teachers coped I don't know. They must have had to rearrange their ideas to accommodate such a vast range of teaching.[110]

The shift system was apparently widespread in other North Wales towns without the added burden of the Ministry of Food families' children. B.W. saw displayed at an open day, decades later, a letter written by his father regarding catchment area.[111] The evacuees that came to the school were accepted where locals had to agitate for places. None of the children minded any disruption through air raids. Some enjoyed the recollections of returning teachers after the war instead of maths lessons. J.L. was displeased with her education which she felt was disrupted greatly by the war, although she had a good job as a legal secretary for 51 years, she felt she could have done much more. She described the mix of children from Manchester, London Ministry of Food and locals from Wales, and their segregation according to the second language they would learn – French, Latin or Welsh respectively. Only those who spoke Welsh at home were allowed to continue due to the shortage of teachers. This underpins the feeling outlined in the *North Wales Weekly News* that evacuation diluted the Welsh language and culture.[112] Temporary huts were built to accommodate the evacuees.[113] Those prefabs that were still there until the 1970s when

J.L.'s son was at school and there was still not the capacity.

> When the children of the Ministry came they had not had the opportunity to take the scholarship in London as it was wartime, as there was no room for them in the Grammar school they came to Pendorlan, so I was with some very clever children, the sort who would have been in the Grammar school. The teachers had to learn a new curriculum altogether.[114]

G.T. describes measures for air raids at primary school. Children were allocated large, middle-class houses for safety, but it was never necessary to go inside or have any contact with the residents. But B.W. remembers:

> There was a siren drill at school we all had gas masks. We were allocated to houses in the area. Yes we did go in sometimes, not just stand at the gate.[115]

One of the boys, B.W., also remembered the raids at night during the Liverpool bombing. Mrs Anne Russell, and her daughter Beryl from next door at the hairdressers on Station Road,[116] went down below her shop to a shelter (cellar), which ran alongside and below Rosie Davies' ladies wear and furrier. B.W. says,

> We went down there too and there was a coke stove heater with fumes that would have been regarded as dangerous today. There was also a coke stove fixed in the classroom at school.

As Dr Wainwright writes, both private secondary schools, Rydal and Penrhos, were requisitioned for office space during the war. The headmistress of Penrhos had connections to the Duke of Devonshire, who then suggested that Penrhos Ladies College would come to Chatsworth (and occupy a place that the army may have otherwise filled). J.B. was a pupil there throughout the war.[117] H.F. went to another private school, Lyndon. She tells how over a weekend in September 1939 the numbers increased by half again. Desks were rearranged to accommodate the Manchester people and the Jews from Cheadham Hill. She says

> All the teachers were being called up so you had different mistresses, very new teachers were coming here so when I came to take my school certificate, I had to go to boarding school.[118]

*Class of College School 1942–3. Hans is 2nd from left 2nd row. [Hans Wins, Antwerp]*

Children of the town at state schools suffered disruption to their education through overcrowding; curriculum would be changed; yet pupils gained a valuable insight of the outside world. Local papers throughout the war show favourable evidence of the impact on theatres and sport, with the participation of the civil servants.

Shops catered to more sophisticated tastes. The impact of war on North Wales was both cultural and economic. The area and people changed and the influence, and the legacy, lasted into the subsequent decades. Even the local football team was successful through the influence of the influx[119] although in other areas football was said never to have regained its popularity during the war due to reduced standards necessarily presented by depleted teams. The local cricket club had been in financial difficulty in the 1930s, but with the input of the military and the Ministry of Food it went from strength to strength during wartime raising £11,704 for five war charities, and an additional fund for the new pavilion. One match in July did so well it raised £5,459 14s 11d.[120]

Hans Wins, a Jewish refugee from Antwerp, was known as 'Dutchie' as the local children did not know the difference between Holland and Belgium. He says:

The first school I attended, [in Colwyn Bay] was College School. It was on the promenade. Coming from the station on Princes Drive turn right onto Marine Drive under the railway bridge towards the promenade. On the left in a slight curve was College School semi facing the beach. On the right was a large dark Victorian type hotel which has been demolished. [Colwyn Bay Hotel] This was a private school run by Mr and Mrs Davies and their daughter Nessie, who also taught at the school. They also had one son who was an army chaplain. I think the school closed because of the age of the headmaster. After that I went to Secondary school in Eirias Park.

I participated in all the school activities, which included prayers, hymn singing, sports etc. Furthermore, I was a keen scout and there were also regular church parades, camping hiking and all the things boys like to do. You could say 'I blended in'. I never found any unfriendliness but on the contrary much compassion. I know that my parents had their worries concerning my sister and one of my brothers who had remained behind in occupied Europe and other relatives who did not survive the Holocaust. I did not realise the seriousness of the situation, it seemed to me a big adventure. I think my parents protected me from this and it was not talked about in my presence. Our house was always open and we had South Africans, Dutch, Belgian and later American soldiers coming in. We enjoyed hospitality and compassion but I am not saying that I never heard 'bloody foreigner' said.

Looking back I am amazed how quickly at a young age one learns a foreign language. There is the grammatical side which is much more difficult but the practical side one learns whilst playing and participating in the usual boyhood pranks! I was well accepted and the teachers made allowances for mistakes I may have made. My fellow classmates, besides the locals, were evacuees from the blitzed cities and from families of civil servants (mostly Ministry of Food). It is here that I received my first 'I love you note' from a girl in the class asking to meet on the corner of Wynnstay Rd and Princes Drive. My father found the note. The girl did not turn up but my father did! Most of my school friends returned to their respective pre-war homes but I am still in contact with some. My very good friend and school mate lived a few houses from us in Bay View Rd, With a group of the school we twice hiked up Snowdon but both times in the clouds with no view!

My brothers had been in the Boy Scout movement and this always fascinated me, you look up to your older brothers. So I joined first the Rhos-on-Sea troop and later the 2nd Colwyn Bay. Not knowing the seriousness of the war situation it all seemed a great adventure and you were only sorry that you were too young to join the forces. (How lucky I was). I was a keen Scout and joined in all their activities. We served as messengers for the Home Guards (who had their H.Q. in Bay View Road.) at mock invasions exercises. On one occasion I had to cycle round the town with a rattle which signalled a 'gas attack' only to fall into the crater and taken to first aid (the crater was just a chalk line in the road which I did not see due to my gas mask fogging up).

Our home was always open and there was much coming and going with a warm welcome to all. I remember soldiers mostly Belgians/Dutch on leave being directed to us. We had some South Africans from the Springbok Regiment that were sent to us from the railway station. An RAF wireless operator showed me how to make me a crystal receiver and later a simple one valve radio. Later the Americans came and next door some US nurses were billeted at Mrs Hughes. They came and spend some evenings with us, how we looked up at their smart uniforms and goodies they brought.

My parents had language difficulties but I know that they much appreciated the understanding and the compassion, which local people showed. They got on well and aside of all their worries they appreciated the kindness and atmosphere, which knit people together in time of need. Yes, they were impressed and very grateful for the warm reception. An anecdote: my father went to the baker Schofields in Sea View Road, it was closed with a note on the window saying that, due to a bereavement in the family, the shop was closed that day. Next day he went in and said 'many more returns of the day' obviously not knowing what 'bereavement' meant. The lady serving must have understood and did not say anything as there were other people in the shop but on a next, quieter day, she explained the mistake and took it in good stride.

I did go several times to the factory and I was always impressed by everything that went on there. I knew the people and, I suppose, was treated as a sort of mascot and spoiled with the little available.

I can only speak about my own experience as seen through the eyes of a teenager. There were many more British Jewish families from the other cities under German bombardment. In Princes Drive they established a Jewish social centre 'Zion House' there was probably also a synagogue.[121]

## Religion and the influx

Before the advent of an increased population, the churches would have served as a social centre, especially for women, most being unemployed. But H.F. testifies that society around church thrived, that the war drew the people into the churches. They were not forgotten and the local people definitely worked together to improve morale with 'Dig for Victory' and various slogans started by the ministry's John Raeburn.

A.D. remembers staff from the Ministry because they went to church and they would be roped in to the parties. Some from London went back after the war but many examples of keeping touch are evident, proving the successful integration.

The mix of religion caused no friction or anti Semitism. D.B. remembers one Jewish boy in the class and was embarrassed when studying *The Merchant of Venice*. Few had heard of the secret Jewish evacuees at Gwrych Castle. A.W. says the taunt from the locals was 'Do you come from Cohen Bay or Llanyidno?' But all children integrated well. The son of the diamond merchant verifies this, and scoutmaster K.D. tells of Jewish refugee children who came into the troop as scouts. There was some difficulty over accepting them into the Methodist building, however Hans Wins said they felt completely welcome. There had also been a Jewish social club on Princes Drive, he claims that eighty-five percent of diamond traders were Jewish.

Some well-to-do families had summer homes in Colwyn Bay as a result of the war. One Jewish family bought a farm in Mochdre and bred pigs to sell. 'They lived on Marine Drive and they were very wealthy. We did not mind the Jews but they stuck together. They kept to themselves.'

The synagogue in Colwyn Bay was said to be probably the only one to ever display the Star of David in the Welsh national colours – red, white and green – in a stained-glass window. It is now preserved in the Gwynedd Archives on the initiative of the late Ivor Wynne Jones and Rona Hart.[122]

## The Ministry of Food

The Ministry of Food transformed and energised the town.[123]

To this day, schoolboys of 1939 still remember when the great influx of people arrived. Several contributors remembered the extent of the requisitioning. But A.R., as an employee of the town information bureau, was witness to the meeting of two civil servants. Bert Fillmore (Senior Executive Officer) and Tim Deeves (Head of Branch) came to implement the dispersal plans and identification of all hotels and boarding houses in the area three months before they arrived in the first week of September 1939. A.R. was himself later employed in the Ministry billeting office before enlisting. The guests had to be cleared, office furniture had to be installed according to instructions found documented. Divisions were Meat and Livestock; Butter and Cheese; Bacon and Ham; Sugar; Cereals; Transport & Warehousing; Tea Coffee and Cocoa; Finance; Billeting; Communications, Animal Feedstuffs, Oils and Fats, Points Rationing, Wartime Meals. A staff distribution list was given to the author by A.R., which he himself had compiled at work after the war when he returned from the navy.[124]

G.T. remembers some of the arrangements for the takeover of so many buildings in 1940.

> Allens fitted out all the hotels. They hoped for the same trade after the war but it did not materialise. All would need refurbishment. The garage in Mochdre had a community room which was given up and taken over as a furniture repository and it dawned on me that the hotels had to deposit their beds and wardrobes somewhere.[125]

A.D. says,

> I don't know if the hotels ever recovered. Because Dad, was in the Police War Reserve during the start of the war and he had to go and empty the hotels of visitors. (Requisitioning) My family also were drapers and they used to go and buy the hotels bed linen from him. But they did not put anybody in the hotels straight away did they, they left them empty. There was one particular lady who never forgave him. My uncle was a builder in the town and he got the job of converting the Colwyn Bay Hotel into offices. The Colwyn Bay Hotel on the promenade was a built of quarry stone. This was where Lord Woolton had his office, which he could reach easily from a track to access the railway.[126]

D.R. applied for a job with Post Office Telephones – 'Yes, Class B release – when you were required back at work it was vital.' A document regarding the ordering of oranges from Spain was discussed with him, and the difficulties of so few phone lines utilised in feeding the nation. The

Ministry succeeded against all odds and the town deserved rather more credit than received, or indeed some credit! Rather than go to the sixth form, D.R. applied to do clerical work with the Ministry. He did not get involved in the social activities as he was only sixteen and lived in Betws-yn-Rhos a few miles out, illustrating that the Ministry needed to recruit so many staff even from outlying areas. A.D. says they did think about altering the time of the buses as children could not get to school at the same time as the Ministry workers.

> I think we went a bit late because of that. Colwyn Bay Hotel was the headquarters of the Ministry of Food. The mail train used to stop for Lord Woolton to get to his hotel at Llandudno Junction.[127]

F.D. says:

> In 1940, in the Summer teenage staff went and signed on at the Ministry but did not admit they would be going back to school in September. Wages were about 19/- a week, which was a lot of money. We did clerical work, figures about bananas, but there weren't supposed to be any bananas were there? I also worked at the Inland Revenue in Llandudno.[128]

J.L. worked for the Ministry of Food at fourteen, addressing envelopes by hand for 'very good money.' 'They were a bit snobby, they [the civil servants] came from London and they thought we were Welsh yobs. There were thousands I think.'[129] But the experience of the individual is varied. A.W. maintains that the integration of the civil servants was absolute and does not recall any problems. When he was fifteen, the personnel department went to the County School looking for staff and he sat an exam and passed. He worked at the Queen's Hotel for Wartime Meals, which organised all the British Restaurants over the country. Later, he was transferred to the Pwllychrochan Hotel and then the Metropole Hotel, where he worked at Eggs Finance. The work consisted of checking orders. After the war his work experience led him to a position in the Salvage Division in Liverpool. The factory sorted animal food from that fit for human consumption at a government depot. Food was brought in from America by boat and graded.[130] Others found employment through word of mouth. G.T. had first to go to Penrhos College for training by a very dour civil-service lady who showed her what was expected of her. She wanted to relocate to London after the war, since her horizons had expanded, but the wage would not have supported her, nor would her parents have approved.

> I was checking accounts. They did not have a list of jobs or work titles; they would just move us on to another table another task. I was in there with two with high ranks but they were civil servants. The wives of the civil servants would be in rooms here so they would not have much to do would they? And everyone had to work. The Ministry moved back to London. It was more convenient for them. It was so fragmented here. I don't know how they ever managed to run it. There was a shortage of paper. We had only 2 or 3 telephones. About 5 in Station Road as they had direct lines to the ports. I was never allowed to use them. They did have porters; message boys taking round from one office to another.[131]

B.W. delivered newspapers to the Ministry.

> The shop assistants had been conscripted therefore we were short staffed. My mother worked there and also a wife of one of the Ministry personnel from London. WH Smith had orders for all the newspapers to go to all the hotels for the Colwyn Bay Hotel, Pwllychrochan, Penrhos College I was a delivery boy. We had far more variety of newspapers in those days, but they would be very thin – thin paper and few pages. *The Sketch; Mirror; Mail; News; Herald; Guardian; Liverpool Post, Birmingham Mail; Express* and *Daily Worker*.[132]

O.R. says:

> I was only 19 at the time and I had to do something. but with my husband at home I had to join the Ministry of Food. I worked for Mr Banks-Amery, he was the head of Retail and Catering, so it was what they had to give out to the restaurants. Everything grew so they were separated in to two branches. Then I became the personal clerk of Mr O'Brian. I could not type or anything but he was always saying to me 'don't you know there is a war on?' and he was there until 7 or 8 every night and he expected me to be there and I should have been making dinner. Well [others] they had their civil servants ways, they clocked off at 6 and they were gone – I could not! When I left in 1943 they all bought me a lamp for the baby. So we really must have got on very well. Wives did not usually work. I know that teachers had to give up when they married.[133]

*Albert and Pat Rigby. Married for 65 years.*

H.F.'s mother by chance met up with somebody on a tram that she was at school with. She had come from the Ministry of Food in London and she had nowhere to live so was invited to live in their granny flat during the war.

She was a Jewish spinster, She worked in the tea division. Tea was stockpiled all over the country as the nation could not do without its beverage. She was an Executive Officer, doing office work, but higher than some people because of her ability. She returned to London when they all disappeared.[134]

Albert says:

Queues at the unemployment exchange were part of the 1938-39 scene. I saw them forming in the early Spring and dispersing soon after the office was opened when it was apparent that there was no work for them. All this was to change within months but for the wrong reasons. I suppose I was too hard up to even consider having a steady girlfriend. Certainly at 16 or 17 we chatted up some of the local girls and met a few holidaymakers. Pat Collins fairground near the Pier Pavilion was a rendezvous for us, not that I can record any real successes. There were dances at the pier in the early weeks of the war started by the Council for young locals and for soldiers who were by now flooding into the area. The first twelve months were for many, many people the most significant they would ever experience. They brought changes no one could ever have contemplated. We did not know what lay ahead.

In Colwyn Bay we hardly knew there was a war on – people went to work as usual, trains ran on time, holidaymakers arrived but we did have to conform to blackout restrictions; we also began to realise that familiar faces were missing as the services made their demands. The orchestra played on the pier, we had no reason to cancel any engagements – it all seemed normal but yet unreal as we listened to our radios and saw the mask drill, ration books were issued, wardens appointed and so on. I wondered how long I would have to wait for call up – the medical would be the first requirement when I would then have to state my preferred service. There was not a doubt in my mind that it would be the Royal Navy but as time went by this seemed uncertain because of the needs of the army.

As I have said we just did not know what lay ahead as we entered the first weeks of the war. To the younger element there was the excitement of change, the uncertainties and the chance for fresh opportunities. Apprehension not fear was the operative word in September 1939; at least this was the prevailing mood in the quiet coastal town of Colwyn Bay. There was quite a large influx of people because it was a reasonably quiet haven – our beaches remained clear, not despoiled with barbed wire and mines and there were few gun implacements – features all too apparent on the south and east coasts.

It was during this bewildering period in the last quarter of 1939 that Pat and I met – at a dance in the Pier Pavilion. This was the first time I had ventured into a ballroom as until then my dancing had been restricted to classes in a small clubroom. Pat, her friend and I sat at first in splendid isolation because hardly anyone else turned up. Johnny Neal the pier manager must have despaired at the lack of response to his efforts to brightening up the early weeks of the war. For me it heralded an important turning point in my life. The following weeks are a delightful blur. Then came our first date and our first kiss on November 18th 1939 and the realisation we were falling in love. An eighteen year old boy and a seventeen year old girl could not have possibly known what love is but we did and so it has remained ever since.

We met more often in succeeding weeks when work permitted and when Pat was not travelling to and from Chester to her ballet school on dimly lit trains through the blackout restrictions. I spent much of my spare time at her mother's guesthouse – an active busy household with a succession of visitors throughout the year. People needed a break and came from far afield for a rest and to enjoy good nourishing meals which were as varied as the rations would permit. Pat's father and uncle had run a successful photographic business for many years, employing a large staff of photographers and darkroom technicians during the summer seasons. The business operated from a studio in Sea View Road. Uncle Frank was a skilled darkroom worker and Pat's dad became a skilled press photographer and his photographs appeared regularly in national and local newspapers. The photographs they produced were of excellent quality and these must be gracing many an album. There is an illustrated book of North

Wales containing many of Pop's photographs. I am sure that in the houses of many Colwyn Bay residents there must be many studio photos bearing the Wrigley stamp and taken in the studio in Sea View Road in the 1920s and 1930s. Others will have retained prints produced from negatives taken at social functions, weddings, operatic and dramatic society shows. One field in which he became expert was in theatrical photography. He produced enlargements for display outside the theatre every week.

Pop was barely making a living with photography when I appeared on the scene and Pat's mother established a boarding house business. Pat was able to remain at ballet school and to gain distinctions. Her eventual success as a ballet teacher gave her parents immense pleasure and they knew I was proud of her as a dancer and supported their aspirations. Nevertheless, the war situation determined the future course of events and it was this, which brought about a change to Pat's intended career.

The first Christmas celebrations of the war was held as usual with a little more poignancy, no one knowing what future Christmases held in store. Rationing had not yet taken full effect so there was no desperate shortage of food. Family gatherings were notable for the absence of some of the young men who were already in the services and of course there were no bright lights in the streets or windows. We arranged a party for our friends as this would be the last time we would all get together before being destined for the Navy and the RAF. We all survived the conflict and came back with different stories and changed ambitions. In the post war years there would be changes to our lives that not one of us would have predicted.

The early months of 1940 brought the realisation that the war would not come to an early conclusion. Instead it would bring distress and sorrow to millions throughout the world. We faced the future with hope. In the Spring of 1940 we heard that Colwyn Bay was to become an evacuation centre on a much larger scale: several groups of children had been evacuated from Liverpool – some stayed for years but most preferred to return to their parents and take their chances when the bombing started. Houses and hotels were being requisitioned for the army and before long we discovered that civil service departments were being moved from London and Colwyn Bay was included in the plan to accommodate them. I worked at the information office for a time and I was loaned to the billeting department. I was involved in the preparatory arrangements to receive the Ministry of Food. Two civil servants came to the advertising office to find out what accommodation was available in the district. The same process was underway in Llandudno with the Inland Revenue eventually monopolising the town. Evacuees, civil servants and others seeking sanctuary in a relatively safe town must have wondered what life would be like in Colwyn Bay. At Rhyl and Prestatyn there were also evacuees but they had to cope with a greater preponderance of troops than we did in Colwyn Bay. Nevertheless British soldiers were billeted in many of the houses and local girls were not long in forming attachments. As time went by there were some girls married to British soldiers abroad who tired of waiting for their men to come back and started liaisons with home based servicemen, civil servants and later with American forces who were stationed in the town prior to the invasion of Europe. Many girls had hopes of a new life-style in the USA – some hopes were realised, many were shattered.

There was a short burst of activity when soldiers arrived direct from Dunkirk. They were confused and bewildered, hurriedly billeted in boarding houses whose landladies had been told by the authorities to turn out their paying guests to make way for the dispirited soldiers The soldiers stayed a couple of days then dispersed, some on leave, some to their units. Disgruntled landladies soon forgot their problems and filled their houses with new guests. Then the civil servants arrived complete with billeting notices – Guinea pigs they were called as for £1 1s. 0d. per week anyone giving accommodation to a civil servant was required to provide a room, bed, breakfast and evening meal. Some of the Ministry staff on low wages did their best to maximise the conditions and paid no more, others supplemented the allowance and got a better service. Very soon men sent for their wives and children, secured rented accommodation and began an enforced sojourn away from bomb-threatened London. They wondered how their London homes were faring during the interminable blitzes. Many wives preferred to brave the conditions and never joined their husbands in Colwyn Bay.

The arrival of the Ministry of Food provided many work opportunities and prospects for local people, far beyond anything they contemplate. For some of us it was another turning point in our lives. It was a strange blend of temporary and permanent staff, and many temps took the opportunity of taking civil service exams when they were re-introduced in 1946. After assisting in the initial billeting arrangements I was recruited as a temporary clerk in the Billeting division of the newly arrived Ministry where I remained as personal assistant to the billeting officer until I joined the Royal Navy. The work was pleasant enough, my colleagues were fine and I made friendships, which continued into the post war years, particularly in Guildford to which the Ministry was dispersed in 1949.[135]

Albert Rigby was the author of *Before We Cross the Bar* and *MMS 172: A Telegraphist's Experience of Wartime Minesweeping* which has had several reprints and is in libraries in Canada, USA, Japan, Belgium and Australia. Rare copies have been sold for £150. Field Marshal Lord Carver asked to use some chapters for his book *The War in Italy 1939-45*. In his civil-service career Albert represented the UK in Brussels, attending Commonwealth conferences at Lancaster House and Marlborough House, visiting the House of Commons and the House of Lords, and being a member of the Balance of Payments Forecasting Committee and the World Economic Prospects Committee for thirteen years. He was photographed with the Lord Mayor of London at the Saddlers Hall in the City, when his books were presented to HMS *Bangor* by the Worshipful Company of Tax Advisors.

The influx of the 5,000 civil servants from London was said by Harry Parker's sister to cause some animosity. They recruited many temporary clerks. The permanent staff were inclined to look down their noses at the temps who were not proper civil servants, but the locals were saying how fortunate they were to have come to this lovely place away from the bombing. The Ministry could not have functioned without the recruitment of the local people like G.R. and Harry's sister. They had to rely on local people, some interviewed who were taken from school e.g. F.D., D.R. – but they would enlist as soon as they were old enough. Some daughters would not be allowed by their fathers to join the WAFs like G.R., or were unable to do so due to health problems like P.B. They therfore had to find alternative employment either in the Ministry, Women's Land Army or munitions. P.B. had never worked and was in her late twenties and had to tell the employment office her that she had been in hospital and could not join up. She went into the department called Wartime Meals, in a section called Queen's Messenger Convoys,

> My uncle warned 'There is a job that you won't like doing and that is reconditioning envelopes!' There were some that would sit and do that all day. They never wasted an envelope, they were opened in a way that they could be used again. I worked for Sir Bertram Chrimes [Wartime Meals] and we did fire watch together. He was good at giving all the staff biscuits from his tin. After he left he was always ready to chat to you if we met on the street. I had a supervisor who was a Grade II Clerk Higher executive officer in the Sugar division, she was from London. I had to draw a graph of the convoys for her, which I enjoyed, but she signed her name to it. It was noticed that she took credit for other peoples' work. Wartime Meals closed down in 1945. But took some time to wind up.

Colwyn Bay Accredited: The Wartime Experience 81

Typists at Mount Royal Ministry of Food Office during wartime (above) and during their reunion in the 1960s (below). [Pat Rigby]

P.B. went to Guildford after the war and followed a civil service career.

> Yes the Ministry of Food moved. 'Bacon and Ham' moved to Stanmore in 1943. I went to Guildford in 1945 when my section closed, (Convoys, at Pwllychrochan Hotel.) I was asked to go to Mount Royal for a meeting and I wondered why. It was because I was being offered a job as an executive officer with the Welfare Foods Department – cod liver oil, milk and orange juice for children – and I stayed there until 1949. I eventually worked locally for the government. I worked at the Metropole Hotel, which became government offices permanently. There were thirty five of us, in four sections - pensions; short term sick pay; contributions and cashiers office.'

This was the social security system recommended by the Beveridge report, which had grown out of observations made during wartime mixing of the classes. I had been talking to PB for over an hour when we realised she had worked with my father in the 1950s and '60s.[136]

> Wartime meals closed down in 1945, and I know because in the next department they were still doing those envelopes. My uncle was in the luxury trade of all stationery, of course it was all gone in the bombing in the Wirral. All that was left was the strong room in the centre of the building. Nothing but rubble and the only thing left standing was the strong room like a little bank.[137] The door was open just a little bit; the Civil Defence man brought out all the records for him [her uncle] his petty cash box was just a mass of black paper. This was a business he had taken over when he had returned from the First World War.

This was something that many of the local people had never experienced. There were very few stray bombs, but bombsites were witnessed in Liverpool in the 1950s.[138]

> There was so much damage it was horrific. There were a great many people evacuated here [Colwyn Bay] some from London some from Liverpool. We had trouble finding a house and did so through the station master who had two sisters. They found a house next door, we were boarders from June 1941. Then Miss Harris heard gossip in church and came after us because a lady was moving to Bexhill because she thought it was safer! We could not believe it! Anyway, she rented her house out for four years. We had our name down with every estate agent and there were no houses to buy. Nothing until the Ministry moved, so even in 1945 people

were desperate for housing We replied to a box number and the lady came to our house to say that even though she had a dining table full of responses to her advert she was coming to us because we were the nearest.

When asked if there was a good social life in the town during wartime P.B. answered 'I saw no difference in the social life, coming from the Wirral'. G.R. remembers the social life.

> They [Ministry of Food] took over Penrhos College There was the social club, that is where you would go to meet people and have a dance. The place would be overrun with Ministry personnel there and there could have been people that you would never even meet? Five thousand from London and all the local people as well. And there were all the soldiers, the Americans. We would be going to Penrhos college all the time, and the Pier. My Mum would not allow me to go out with just anyone. She said 'bring them back'. They were good days then. I worked with Londoners who were very nice. My division was called 'Eggs Finance'. I would be writing cheques for all over the country for different bodies. I did not have anything to do with the rationing. I started at 8 am and worked until 6pm we entered by the fire escape at the back. We were well paid. I think about £3 a week. And there was a house where you could go and have your lunch. I went there a few times. When I got married I was still in the Ministry of Food, hoping to work there for two more years.

A.D. & F.D. remember the British Restaurants where you could get meals, three courses with roast lamb, pudding and coffee for one shilling [five pence]. There was also the British Restaurant at the Congregational church.[139]

D.B.'s aunt took a civil service exam, and at the end of the war went to Guildford and got a pension.[140] Of those 5,000 Londoners entering the town it would have been a big percentage of the original population in those days, twenty-five percent, without taking into account other influx.[141] Even with the civil servants and junior clerks recruited at every opportunity including the schools it was still necessary to bring in juniors from outlying district such as Betwys, as in the case of D.R.

### A civil service family[142]

B.D. spoke about her trip to the south of England when the department she worked with, 'Butter and Cheese', returned to Stanmore in 1946.

I went back in 1946 and we had a special train to take us to Stanmore. Lachlan McLean from the Home Guard was still working there until 1947, but I went in 1946 with the 'Butter and Cheese' section. They wanted us to train their staff, because a lot of them did not go and you can't stop the Ministry just because the war stopped. We travelled by train.

She showed two letters written to her by Ministry staff, one when she had first started and the other when she left. M.H. remembered her boss was in the Home Guard and that he was of high rank, Lachlan MacLean, OBE. His name appears in the book *Bureaucrats in Battledress*. M.H. said 'The higher-rank CO and EO and then HEO and SEO, and any above and EO they would become officers.'

B.D. spoke of her colleagues, 'They were all Londoners, the originals, and they would say that here it was always raining and that it was lovely weather down south. I must have been there about three months.' Sadly B.D. thought that none of them would still be alive now because they were all in their forties back then. She remembered that when the civil servants came up it was only a small Ministry and, with the war and with all the rationing and supplies coming in from abroad, they had to recruit locally so there must have been hundreds of staff to manage all the work there was to do. It was rather tricky to track down those remaining and without networking and recommendations it would have been impossible. There had been so many in wartime filling all the buildings in the town.

'Yes,' remembered M.H.

> ... there were thirty eight hotels, then there was Penrhos college and Rydal. I was in the 'Pwllychrochan hotel'. And then there was the Metropole – that was the finance department where they did the salaries. And all those hotels like Mount Stewart – they were all full. The offshoot was 'Westfield'. My sister was comptometer operator in that red-brick building in Pwllychrochan Avenue. When I came back I went to Wartime Meals division they sent me an invitation to a farewell party in 1947. They were clearing it all up then. They did all these British Restaurants and the equipment, and when I went back I went into 'Establishments' in Colwyn Bay Hotel. And in a photograph ... this lady here [ shows photograph] was my boss. She went to Guildford. and this card was from her.

Some went to Guildford and continued their careers, like P.B. who had been interviewed earlier:

I worked with her in Wartime Meals. And then we worked in the DSS [Department of Social Security]. She had never worked you see she lived with her aunt she was 28 when she started so that was her war work. We both worked with your father in the Metropole buildings after the war.

B.D. said,

Bob, your Dad, was in insurance before he joined the Ministry of Pensions – yes the Prudential.
'There are still some old Colwyn Bay-ites living in Guildford, Married and retired, my age. Agriculture fisheries and food now isn't it? They are still there around Merrow and Burpham.

B.D. and M.H. suggested I advertise in the Guildford area. I had already met J.M. and M.M., a couple who had relocated. One of my best friends was born in Guildford, to a relocated Ministry worker, John Vaughan, who is in the ATC photograph.

'Lots of these people who went to Guildford like PB eventually came back here and if there were jobs that's how they got into the Ministry of Pensions. P.B. was cashier. You know she is 97?

'Yes,' I answered,' she had just had her birthday the day before I interviewed her.'

B.D. went on 'She organises all our civil service trips and her writing can put kids to shame these days – mind you my mother's – and M.H.'s mother were the same – and M.H.'s was 88 when she died.'

P.B. was an interesting lady, with her story. Most efficient, and still as efficient now as when she was then with her organisational skills. P.B. has since told me that the 'Civil Service Fellowship' is no longer running due to loss of so many members'.

B.D. had a story to tell.

What I always think was amazing was when I went for the interview from the grammar school [which was then called the County School] I went to Pwllychrochan, there was a lady there chatting away to me asking what I had done at school and then she said to me – 'Its an unusual name.' – I replied ' oh yes, my grandfather was Austrian – Tuczek and she said I've never heard it before but I remember just after the first World War – she had been in the Ministry of Labour and transferred to the Ministry of Food because of the war and she said a Captain Wenzel Tuczek interviewed me for a job in the Ministry of labour. And I could not believe it! This was in 1943 and it had been 1919 when he had interviewed her for a job! for a secretarial job after he was in the war, then he worked for the civil service. My father started that camp for the unemployed at Capel Curig. He also did one at Suffolk. He was in Port Sunlight then we went to Suffolk because he had been in the army in the Battle of the Somme. It was really like a army camp with 200–300 unemployed, they had come from all over. She could not believe it – but it wasn't only four or five years ago when you think it was the First World War.

M.H. also had a story, and said,

> The only interview I remember was when in 1941 I went to work for a chartered accountant who brought all the officers from Ipswich to Colwyn Bay to do all the wages for the farmers. By 1941 they decided to go back to Ipswich, there was no danger from bombs ... so they thought. So I went to the interview at the 'Rothsay' for the Ministry of Food and sat down and you had to fill a form for official secrets and all that. There was something I did not understand so I nervously asked a man who was sitting next to me and it was ' have you ever been in any ... pecuniary difficulties ...?' He explained and I never saw him again. I filled in the form and I got the job. Handling money? Oh yes, so they asked all these sort of questions.'

'What else did they ask you?'
'Well, your education?'

B.D. and M.H. agreed that there is nothing written anywhere about any of this, and feel that the town did not get enough credit for its contribution to the war effort. They remembered:

> It was quite an upheaval. It ruined the tourist trade ... never got back to normal, holiday makers used to come to the small boarding houses. Apart from the Ministry, many came from Manchester ... came to escape the bombing.

BD lived on Church Drive and remembered that there were many Jewish families. With the civil service the family used to rent houses. She remembered when her father came here first to look for a house in Colwyn Bay, there were over 500 empty houses here then for rent just before the war– he came in 1938 before the war, and then during the war not only the Ministry were here but the soldiers were here too, billeted all over.' I remembered what PB had said about the difficulties she had had finding a house to rent during the war, and evident by all the 'wanted' ads in the local paper of the day.

M.H. remembered one hotel, West Point, 'They [the Americans} must have thought they were at home at West Point. The Royal Signals had already left and gone to the Middle East.'

B.D. continued:

> When the Ministry of Food came it absolutely blossomed because they had to get staff – so it was ideal because it wasn't an area where there was employment except for hotels – especially for women – it was a boon really ... well paid. Civil servants jobs were the cream of jobs then absolutely– its very different now.' Her daughter is in the Civil Service - third generation. Her husband was also a civil servant, and her brother. 'He went into the admiralty from school but then left and went into teaching. Physics and Maths. My sister, was in the civil service, my other brother was in the Ministry of Defence, my uncle now in South Africa was in Tavistock Square, head of Ministry of Labour, it was a family thing and a safe job.'

A question.'Was it OK for married women to continue working after they were married?'

'Oh yes, married women were able to continue after marriage'.

I was surprised at this answer as I explained about the marriage records and no disclosure of occupation.

'Before the war the women teachers weren't allowed to stay on. They [civil servants] came in single, they married, and they stayed on and continued to work. I did, and so did M.H.'

'What did you put on your marriage certificate?'

'Can't remember'

> We were saying we had all these clubs and we used to have dances, music, cycling. The war brought a lot of culture to the area. Everybody seemed to get on. From Liverpool, Manchester, London and Welsh and the Americans and they all got on. Right through the country. This is what is so sad – then everybody helped everybody. They, all came to this quiet place and had to get on. Churches were crowded with civil servants.
> I was 13 when war broke out in 1939 and then we had Blackburn High School for Girls came here evacuated from Liverpool. I got the scholarship and we used to go to school in the morning, Blackburn High School girls

would be there. And then we had to go on Saturday morning it was quite amazing really in fact one of my best friends, she stayed on. I took my school certificate in 1940 we were only going to school part time for a year. Shifts operated in school – too many pupils. As we were on shifts we left little notes for the girls, we never met them they sat in our desks in the afternoon. But it disrupted my education. The headmaster, Mr Dodd, went white in the course of a year. It was a terrible strain. It was the time of Dunkirk. We all had disruptions in one way or another.

How did they cope with the different levels of education?

They had brought their own teachers so they had their own classes you see. Some of our masters had gone in the army, anyway it was very very different but they all pulled together.

You know the government buildings on Bryn Euryn – were built as an emergency hospital originally, then they put 'Meat and Livestock' [a department] in there. There's still government in there. Driving test centre. I think.

'The war had a great impact on all avenues of society. Were you aware of any other contributions the town made towards the war? Industries?

'Well they used to do munitions in Mochdre didn't they? We were never really informed about what was going on until after the war. It wasn't until I read the book after the war about Mulberry Harbour'.

Did not you know about the bombs which had fallen on Dinerth Road? Did you feel in danger at all?

'No. No, you did not feel it. The bombers used to fly over here to Liverpool and there was a peculiar sound, Messerschmitts and you could see Liverpool burning'.

A lot of people have said that.

On Dinerth Road was a time bomb and you know the Royal Mail train used to go through and they reckon when it picked up the mail it never stopped but opened the door and some light escaped and it was probably a bit of light from that and they dropped a bomb. No one felt or realised danger when they were young.

And they used to practice because they used to have boats and targets – in case anyone landed here. Our neighbours used to invite soldiers who were billeted in boarding houses and have the boys in for baths and for tea. My mother had one with asthma so he had to go to the sick bay – Crossley

Mount on Whitehall Road, for the troops, on the corner of the road opposite the old vegetarian home [hotel, lodging, billet]. You did not realise there were so many hotels in the town.

We used to work at the Toc H canteen Thursday and Saturday at Douglas Road Comrades Club. They had dances they called the 'local hop' and the swimming pool in Rhos – lovely ballroom.

M.H. was born in Glan Conwy in 1925. B.D. came in 1938.

We came from Suffolk, and before that from Manchester to Suffolk. But, before I was born, my brother and sister were born in London, then they came to Manchester. Actually we were very lucky because we missed the war. When the war broke out my father was transferred down to London and he was in the ARP down there. It was terrible down there.

M.H.'s father died – he was a civil engineer with McAlpines and worked on big contracts in Scotland and building roads, and in the Midlands, building aircraft factories. He was in the bombing in Coventry, caught pneumonia and died 1942. We did not have any drugs in those days – there were drugs ... but only for the forces, not for ordinary people, we only had to do home nursing.

When you think about how this place has grown here, its only since the war, it was very quiet, it was all cornfields. A lot of people did not go back – and they are still coming in. They got jobs and then eventually the older ones retired. M.H. went away in 1946, got married, and then came back here twenty years ago.

Like my brother, he was in National Service, then into the bank and then into teaching. In Crewe and Corshsam High School, and his wife was a teacher and she came from round here and they returned here. When you think of people in Manchester and London you can't blame them for coming back.

M.H. said they always attended the Civil Service Clerical Association and belonged to the Red Cross as well. At the beginning of the war the billeting office came round and did not force you, but you had to take them and my mother had six bedrooms so we had to fill them.

> Colwyn Bay was awash with all sorts of troops. I met my husband when he was billeted with my friends in Old Colwyn. My husband's regiment was in South Wales for a while. He was in the battle of Casino and Italy was quite similar to Wales [the terrain] and I could see why they would practise in Wales. He died in 1984.

M.H. has a reproduction copy of the 1895 *North Wales Weekly News*, issued on the centenary in 1995. She said how interesting it was to see all the hotels and shops advertised. Hotels used to issue the guest list, the Cartmell Hotel was mentioned. We spoke of St Mary's College, which has been demolished. The Butter and Cheese Department was in the building where Rydal is now (Pwllychrochan Hotel), where B.D. worked during the war.

'What did you have to do involving butter and cheese?'

> Well obviously it used to come in from Australia and New Zealand and we used to have these big lists and we had the proforma invoices from the New Zealand Star, the Australia Star all these different ships and we used to have advice notices with so many tons of butter and cheese …

M.H.

> … and these were sent to my department, statistics intelligence, and we would gather so many how we knew exactly how many, every grain of corn and know how much of everything. That's where the statistics and intelligence came in.

'Did you have to go on a course to learn how to do this work?

> No, it was clerical work. And also, when it came in we had all these huge ledgers of all the cold stores in the country. There is one at the junction. Meat and butter and cheese were stored all over the country, and we would have a page for each of the ships and where it was coming from. No computers no calculators and no e mail. Hardly any telephone lines and also no paper and all so efficient. The whole country.
>
> And apart from feeding our own people we were feeding all those that had come in like all these Jewish people from Germany, and do you know it was like the invasion.
>
> The only other bit of war work I did was that they used to issue, the government to everyone under 21 was 'NAMCO' – National Milk and Cocoa. Usually the junior – it was usually me – would make this for all the under nineteens, instant cocoa with vitamins.
>
> Yes, that was my job too, making it for everyone, and they were in big gold tins. It was a lovely drink, a bit like the instant chocolate now. And that was free to us. I used to do all the accounts for that. I had forgotten about that. I did have one of the tins for a long time. It was all part of keeping us fit.

'Oh yes, and you had to grow your own vegetables'. Digging up your lawns to dig for victory? John Raeburn, who instigated the 'Dig for Victory' campaign, was discussed, and how Colwyn Bay was never mentioned in his obituary. M.H. has to go now, and sends regards to Albert Rigby, another contributor.

## The Diamond Industry

A refugee family from Antwerp in Belgium opened a diamond factory in Colwyn Bay, dramatically increasing the contribution of the town to the war effort. During the war the diamond industry was of strategic importance not only for supplying diamond impregnated and diamond tipped tools necessary for manufacturing war material but also as a payment vehicle for the 'Lend-Lease' agreements with America for armaments. The demand for diamonds grew dramatically because of their negotiating value and facility of transport. Germany was prevented from acquiring industrial diamonds vital for industry.

*Articles of Association. Letter advising Gerrit Wins of permission to establish the diamond tool factory, Frisch & Wins, in Colwyn Bay, 1940. [Hans Wins, Antwerp]*

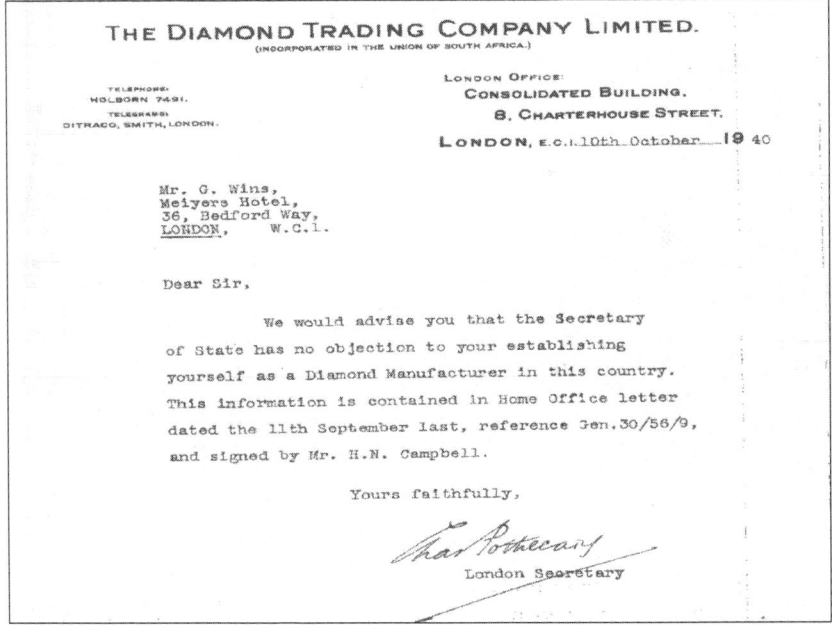

As a Boy Scout Hans, son of the founder of the factory, wrote the memoir of his escape as a teenager during the war in the *Steadfast Gazette*.[143] It was a very exciting time for a young boy in those days. What was even more exciting was that Hans' father, Gerrit Wins, was carrying a briefcase of diamonds during the escape. The French army gave the family preferential treatment for a safe passage. Hans, maintains that the film *Operation Amsterdam* romanticises the tale of the escape with the diamonds. He was a young schoolboy who had a similar experience of escape with his family from Belgium in 1940. He describes the exciting and dangerous journey through France and across the channel to Falmouth, at one time climbing a rope ladder, with his father who was carrying a briefcase containing diamonds.[144] After a few months in London during the Blitz, where Hans learned an elementary standard of English, the family eventually settled in Colwyn Bay. Older brother, Leo, had joined the Princess Irene Brigade, comprising mainly of Dutchmen and stationed in the vicinity of Conwy, which was, of course, very peaceful compared to the blitzed cities. When asked the reasons for establishing the diamond factory in Colwyn Bay Hans says that it was known to be a peaceful area where you would not believe there was a war going on.

We rented a furnished flat on the first floor of Clifton House, 9 Bay View Road. The second floor was rented by another refugee family, Max Frisch, also from Antwerp and a business associate of Gerrit Wins.

*Examples of the machine tools used in the diamond factory.*

[Hans' father] They founded the firm of Frisch & Wins of which Hans has the original Articles of Association. Mrs Anna Frisch was actually the secretary at the factory because of her excellent command of the English language.

The factory was opened on Princes Drive on the top floor of the Bevan's Building. Bevan's ironmongery was on the ground floor. Hans Wins is anxious to find a photograph of the exterior of that building for an exhibition in Belgium. In 2010, an exhibition was set up in the local library, and an appeal made for residents to come forward with further information, memories and artefacts. A jeweller encountered perusing the exhibition claimed he had a file of industrial diamonds obtained from the Frisch & Wins factory. T.M., from Llandudno, remembered the heavy safe adjacent to the building, built in an Egyptian style.[145] Children of the Conwy Road School visited with the Mayor to view the cabinet and the mayor started a competition, providing prizes for the best piece of work the children could create concerning anything they could find out about the wartime diamond manufacture.

As in all 'diamond families', the talk was always about cutting techniques, new equipment, rough-diamond supplies, etc. It was a close circle and, as always in times of need and danger, closely knit.

'You needed each other?'

> Yes, I did visit the factory and I was fascinated by the work going on. I particularly liked a Ritchie Roberts who lived in Llandudno Junction. He was a carpenter by profession and was generally the handy man at the factory and also did the scouring of the scaifes [polishing wheels]. I remember him because he used to make model planes for me. As for the other cutters most of them came to the house and some I remember.[146]

G.R., still a local resident, remembers working in the factory as a teenager. She says she was the only woman working in the office where she was employed to set the stones in the 'dops'. What she remembers about the work was the cutting of the diamonds in half. She says 'they were industrial diamonds like in a watch, but these would be dull and would be about as long as your finger. The only thing that would cut a diamond is another diamond and the noise would be horrendous. They would be used in planes for navigation instruments [and high precision tooling for aircraft

*Opening of the diamond factory, 31 July 1941. The Mayor and Mayoress are evident in the centre of the photograph. Left of the Mayor is Mr Thorpe, a tobacconist from Abergele Road, who was also an auxiliary policeman. To the left of Mr Thorpe, wearing glasses, is Mr Bialoskiersky, known as 'Biallo'. Mr J. C. Williams is just behind the Mayor's shoulder. Mrs Anna Frisch is standing next to the Mayoress and, just behind the two ladies, is Gerrit Wins, Hans' father. [Hans Wins, Antwerp]*

engines as well as dies for drawing filaments]'. As a young girl, G.R. was not given permission by her parents to join the Wrens, and as the manager of the diamond factory was a lodger with the family, he gave her a job. Others employed in the factory enjoyed the status of being in a reserved occupation and would therefore not be called up for military service.[147]

The tools and machinery for diamond cutting were not available in the UK and the few that were, ran out. The manufacture of these tools was almost monopolised by Belgium. Diamond-sawing machines were also made by Slamco in the USA, from where they were ordered. The first shipment was destroyed in a bombing raid on Liverpool. A second shipment did come through. It was difficult to get cargo space on convoys primarily reserved for war material and badly needed food. Polishing

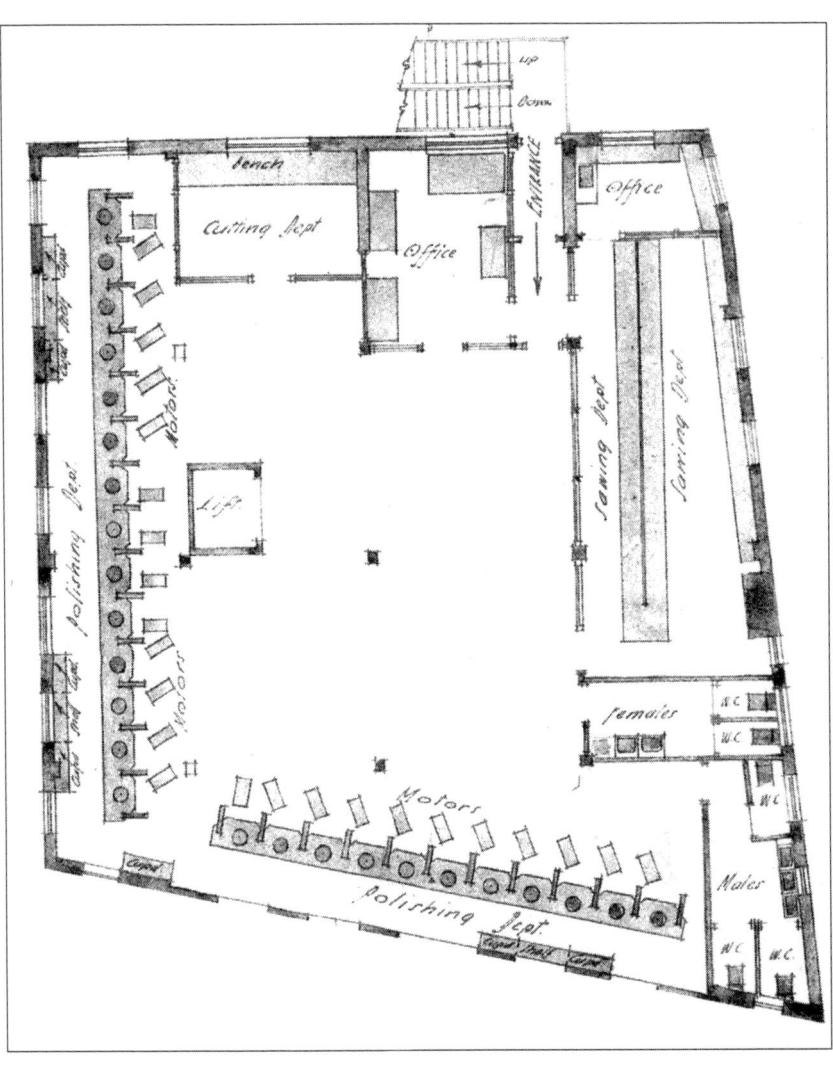

*Floor plan of the diamond factory. [Hans Wins]*

*The Mayor of Colwyn Bay, Abdul Khan, in 2010, with children of Conwy Road School who came to see the diamond industry exhibition, and the author.*
*[Helen Jackson photographer]*

*Hans Wins with Mrs Roberts, a wartime employee of the diamond factory.*
*[Hans Wins, Antwerp]*

*Frish & Wins personnel. Standing (L–R): Charles Elders, Jack Ziekenopaser (Raphael) and Eddy de Clerck. Sitting on the left is Mrs Elders and Sonja Raphael is in the centre; others unknown. Mr & Mrs Elders lived on East Parade. They had a son born in Colwyn Bay. A pram could not be found, but Hans Wins found one in the bicycle shop on Abergele Road. Mr Elder was a diamond cutter. Mrs Elders was from Ostende and it was in her father's fishing boat that they escaped to Britain, landing in Swansea (where most of the Belgian fishing fleet was based during the war).*

*Jack Ziekenopaser changed his name to Raphael on arrival in Britain. He was a diamond cleaver and had a little workshop at his house in Woodlands Road. Sonja was his daughter. Jack taught some of his skills to Leo, Hans Wins' older brother, and to Hans as a schoolboy. Eddy de Clerck developed a portable machine for desalinating sea water.*

wheels were made by an engineering firm called Asquith and other tools were made locally by Mr Dua and Mr Stoeltjes, Belgian refugees.

The Colwyn Bay diamond factory, as well as those in Bangor, contributed greatly to the war effort through its manufacture of diamond tools for navigation instruments. Hans Wins is still very involved in the diamond industry in Antwerp, Belgium. He still has a great fondness for the town of Colwyn Bay and keeps in touch with old friends and has returned to visit many times.[148]

## 7: Contributions from civil servants from other areas of the UK during the war.

> I hated it when the German planes used to go over to bomb Liverpool, where I had relatives. Surprisingly, they never dropped a bomb on Colwyn Bay, though they could have done a lot of damage to the food supply had they done so. [M.L.H.]

It was interesting to get an alternative perspective from those who came into the town and not just the locals, but how to find them? I discovered from a conversation at a wedding that Wynne Jones, now in her nineties, had moved from Saville Row, London, as personal assistant to Sir William Duffy, head of the Bread Division. Her name must have helped her to fit in well with the locals in Rhos-on-Sea. She brought her sister, and her tiny nephew, whose surname was Edwards, and they stayed until the baby was four-years old. That baby was the ex brother-in law of my partner.

It was at the suggestion of a former mayor of Colwyn Bay, Mrs Laurette Danson that I wrote to a magazine, which included a page of 'reunions.' The letter was edited down and lost its original meaning, and I hope the respondents were not too disappointed that there was not an actual reunion of civil servants from the 1940s,

Margaret answered the request in which I wrote that I was hoping to find anyone who had worked at the Ministry in Colwyn Bay during wartime. She said she had considerable nostalgia for her five years in Colwyn Bay. By coincidence I found that she is the grandmother of a boy who was at school with my son in Surrey from 1992 to 1998, I had met her daughter at the school gates, but never realised the connection. Margaret recalls her experiences in a letter to me. I later visited her at home.

*Margaret Harvey (née Lloyd)*
> I was just sixteen when I was evacuated to Colwyn Bay in 1940 with my father who worked for the Ministry of Food, having been 'borrowed' from

Unilever to staff the Oils and Fats division. He had asked if there would be a job for me and was told it would be better for me to join the Ministry of Food in London, rather than later in Colwyn Bay, as I would get the financial benefits of being evacuated, which I did. My mother and my younger brother were to follow on when we found suitable accommodation.

Initially I was billeted on two elderly ladies, who lived in a bungalow in Old Colwyn. They seemed quite pleased with whom they had 'got' (as I heard them discussing it with neighbours!) and they made quite a fuss of me. My father wasn't so lucky. His billet was in a boarding house in the Bay with several other men, run by a typical Manchester landlady who, like most of the other landladies, was not at all pleased at having had to cancel her summer visitors to accommodate civil servants at a guinea a week, bed breakfast and evening meal! Though my Dad said she had made the most wonderful rice pudding – except they had it every day!

The Oils and Fats [department] were housed in the Pwllychrochan Hotel situated at the top of a long steep hill and I also worked there in the typing pool. Eventually they moved to the Colwyn Bay Hotel on the seafront and I moved to the Legal and Enforcement Department when they split. Here I was personal assistant to the Head of Animal Feedstuffs. We had a team of inspectors who toured the country randomly visiting farms to check if food fit for human consumption was being fed to livestock. If they found flour etc. in animal feed bins the hapless farmer was prosecuted and we prepared the instructions to prosecute to send to the CPS. I stayed with that department at Ellesmere for the rest of my time in Colwyn Bay.

As to accommodation, we found rooms in the Bay with a Welsh family, who were wonderful – it helped that my father was Welsh, though he had left Llangollen as a youth to find work in Liverpool, with Unilever. There was Mr and Mrs Hughes, Fred who was the same age as my brother, and they went to Old Colwyn Grammar School together and became lifelong friends. There were also Rosina and Eirlys, two younger girls with whom I am still in touch. There was also Auntie (Mrs Hughes) a very small wrinkled old lady in her eighties who only spoke Welsh but said, '*Oh, Peggy bach*' and hugged me when we met in the hallway.

Sadly, my mother died from cancer in 1943 after a traumatic year in and out of Colwyn Bay Hospital and several operations. Mrs Hughes helped nurse her during the time she was at home and was always producing items of unrationed food, the occasional egg, a rabbit (which I had to skin) and a bit of farm butter from her brother's farm in Llanrwst, which she thought my mother might eat. After my mother died and I became chief cook and bottle washer (very inexperienced), the Hughes family helped me so much.

Apart from the sadness over my mother, I loved my stay in Wales, especially my job. We were such a compatible crowd. Even our weekly fire watch was fun though the camp beds weren't very comfortable! Though I hated it when the German planes used to go over to bomb Liverpool, where I had relatives. Surprisingly, they never dropped a bomb on Colwyn Bay, though they could have done a lot of damage to the food supply had they done so.

The Enforcement department was disbanded at the end of the war and the Oils and Fats quickly returned to London. I kept in touch with some of my old colleagues for a while and actually bumped into my old boss in Sainbury's in Surbiton one day (this would have been in the 1960s). I must have been one of the youngest members of staff to be evacuated from London and was certainly the youngest in my department. I am now 85 and I can't imagine there are many of the original evacuees still alive.

*Alec Parselle*, MBE

I was able to communicate with, the son of the late Alexander Reginald Parselle, after he wrote to me in response to the same request for information. Alec, as he was known, was born in London but had a south-west Wales background.[149] He was posted from London to Colwyn Bay in August 1940 and was a Principal Officer (now known as a Grade 7) and the

*Home Guard standing at ease on the Promenade, Colwyn Bay. Reproduced from* Bureaucrats in Battldress, *Henry Smith, 1945.*
*[Mrs Ann Smith, grand-daughter of the battalion photographer Corporal A. Wrigley]*

## Ode to No. 10 Platoon, B Company, 11th Denbighshire Battalion

I hymn the praise of No.10, the flower of 11th Den,
The sweepings of the Nation's Jails, blot upon the North of Wales,
Well versed in drilling N & D, uncouth unto the nth degree,
Proficiency is more displayed in pontoon school than on parade.

There leads this motley spawn of hell a bashful officer, Parselle,
A beardless boy, a flappers' feast he's a poor wee timorous cowering beastie.
When first he forced us on parade he stammered, hopelessly dismayed,
'I doubt you'll harm the enemy but Oh by …. You frighten me.'

We have a sergeant cursed by God, his form disfigured by perpetual pod
His golf the worst that o'er ploughed up a green does not excuse his stories so obscene.
His voice like starter, loud but apt to loiter, his [bost] heaves above a brewer's goitre.

An N.C.O in our platoon wears wings upon his chest,
I dread to look for fear of harm on his equine face devoid of charm
His chest and feet so small and flat he's thin and weedy like Jack Sprat,
His hair is sparse, few brains beneath, he hasn't even cut his teeth.

We've a hairy legal corporal just lately started breeding,
His wife has burnt his book by Marie Stopes that he was reading.
His his two striped he was rather proud of,
But he's failed you'll all agree,
To apply the laws of nature and increase them into three.

We've a lance Jack long and stringy who's the bookie's sole support
Though he's dallied with the maidens we're afraid he'll soon be caught
We've a [.....] little Taffy
Name of Private Frankie Owen
Though he says that he's teatotal well I really can't be knowing.

I never in my wildest dreams imagined such a lot,
We've accountants and some honest men, and B……. who's not,
We've a Private Paul so positive that he would run the sector
And a sergeant who was, God knows why, made Auditing Director.
We've a senior costings officer and really must admit
He's nothing but a downright drunken, noisy little ……
He keeps the Central going seldom smelling like a rose,
He can guess why Grecian Helen scratched his handsome Roman nose,

And that is our platoon boys, and I swear by all the gods,
They're the finest and most soldierly of all MacLean's poor sods.

Anon

*Ode to No. 10 Platoon, B Company, 11th Denbighshire Home Guard Battalion*
*[Geoff Parselle]*

head of his department in the Meat and Livestock Division and was a specialist in the transporting of animals. He was also involved in the storage of meat (corned beef mainly) in buffer depots where millions of tins of this and other meat were stored for emergency use. He and his wife Ceinwen (from Mountain Ash) stayed in the town until 1947, and their only child Geoff was born in a Colwyn Bay nursing home in 1945. Geoff himself worked as a professional photographer both in the RAF (for fourteen years) and for thirty years in the Ministry of Defence. He sent me photos of his father in the Ministry Battalion of the Home Guard in Colwyn Bay, including the anniversary parade through Colwyn Bay on 16 May 1943. This shows Alec saluting and zone commander Colonel Barton taking the salute. There is also a photograph of the presentation of the proficiency cup by Colonel Llewellin from the Ministry of Food south of View Point Colwyn Bay. This appears in the book *Beaurocrats in Battledress*. But a song entitled 'Ode to No. 10 Platoon, B Company, 11th Denbighshire Battalion,' is not previously published.

Alec had enrolled in the Local Defence Volunteers of the Ministry of Food when it was formed in 1940 and when it moved to Colwyn Bay and became F Company of the 1st Battalion of the Home Guard he became a

*Colonel Barton taking the salute from Alec Parselle. [Geoff Parselle]*

lieutenant and platoon officer in 5 Platoon. He was allowed to wear the flash of the Royal Welch Fusiliers. In May 1942, the Company decided to form its own mobile column and soon after, in January 1943, its own 11th Battalion. Alec Parselle succeeded a Lt Hooker in command of the Mobile Column and stayed with them until its closure in July 1945. He was at one time also platoon officer of No. 10 Platoon, B Company. His platoon won the battalion Proficiency Cup in 1944, and Geoff has it on display at home.

In 1947, Alec was transferred and the family moved to New Malden in Surrey. He stayed with the Ministry, which became the Ministry of Agriculture, Fisheries and Food in London (Whitehall) and then in Tolworth. He received the MBE from the Queen in 1953 for his work. He retired to Somerset in 1972. Geoff remembers that his father used to travel around the country sorting out transport and food storage problems and spent some of his time around Liverpool docks where most of our food from the USA came in. He was very much a transport specialist for food and became an associate member of the Institute of Transport on the 17 September 1940.

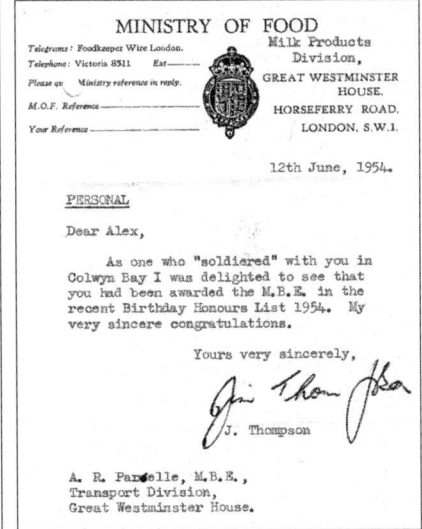

*Letters of congratulation from Lachlan MacLean (left) and J. Thompson (above) to Alec Parselle. [Geoff Parselle]*

Mr Alex Reginald Parselle of 55 Hollington Crescent New Malden, who is assistant director of the Transport Division of the Ministry of Food has been made an MBE. At one time with the, then, Great Western Railway on clerical duties, he joined the Bacon Marketing Board in 1938 and was absorbed in to the Ministry of Food during the war when he was in the Bacon and Ham Division. He has been responsible for the distribution of food both during and since the war and secured his present appointment in 1947. He gained his B.Sc. (Econ) degree at the University of London in 1937. Mr Parselle has lived in Malden since 1947 having previously lived in Ewell. He is married and has a son at Malden Manor School. Mr Parselle, who is 48, is a member of the school's parents association.[150]

*Mrs Mairwen Roberts*
Mrs Roberts of Mold said she was flabbergasted to read the letter in the magazine requesting input. She joined the Ministry in 1941 having left a teacher-training college and having to make a decision between the armed forces and the civil service. She traveled by train from her home in Bangor every day and served first as a sports and social secretary, but soon went into the statistics department. She was fortunate enough to be chosen to go to Cambridge on a statistics course and gained a 2nd Class diploma which stood her in good stead when she returned to Colwyn Bay. She left to get married in 1946, although she was offered a post in London. It was she who suggested to Marjorie McAleese, that she could write and contribute her story.

*Marjorie McAleese*
Marjorie, born in 1922, wrote from Essex after hearing about the request for information in the magazine from Mairwen Roberts, and although partially sighted, wrote a cover letter herself and also completed a questionnaire in her own writing. She claimed that to a partially Welsh-speaking town, the impact was enormous. She remembers some of the evacuated staff going to America as G.I. brides. She thinks the attitudes of women changed greatly; it was really the emancipation of women. She lost a member of her family who died aged 19 in the services. Her sister was a secretary and her father a manager of a large engineering works that manufactured rubber.

I left school in July 1939 having applied to the Civil Service in May, reluctantly as it was my father's wish, as war was imminent and he feared that girls could be sent away to work on munitions.

I was called to London from Watford, my home town, to Food Defence Plans at Great Westminster House on 30 August 1939 and was taken on as Clerical Assistant to start immediately. I traveled to London every day by train (Monday to Friday) my wages were 27/6d per week.

At Christmas that year we became the Ministry of Food and were to be evacuated to Colwyn Bay to work on dietary necessities per person, to develop a ration book. We were evacuated around April. At the station we were all given addresses of our billets and taken there. Army beds and blankets were provided, mainly two to four per room. It was a shock on both sides as very few of us, (mainly young females from good families,) some like me had never been away from home, even for one night. Integrating was difficult, sharing rooms with strangers and having landladies who would lapse into Welsh when we appeared.

We were billeted in various hotels, guest houses and schools in the area. Colwyn Bay hotel was offices, as was Station Road Hotel, the Rothesay Hotel and Rydal boys' school. Penrhos girls' school was a canteen, offices, social space and a large hall for dancing and superb sports facilities. Silver Howe Hotel was a sick bay. Westfield Hotel was part offices, part domestic, ironing, etc. The Methodist Guest Home, Plas-y-Coed was a billet for about 70 females some in dormitories and some in rooms for two or three. I was lucky to move to Plas-y-Coed after several indifferent lodgings. There was a resident hostess and we had to sign 'in and out'. She met any boyfriends and arranged supervisory dances in the ballroom. There was only one girl sent home pregnant. We were very lucky that Mrs Abel took her responsibilities very seriously. Local churches welcomed us warmly, C of E, Catholic, Congregational and Presbyterian. I soon picked up my Sunday school teaching with newly found friends from the church. We opened a very successful youth club. I am still in touch with our pianist there, now 92, and in a home in Colwyn Bay.

Leave to go home was one week, twice a year. Not all went back home so family life was changed, more than from the service people who still went back home on each leave. Inevitably it changed our lives. So many of us met our future husbands. I met the man I was to marry who was in the RAF and stationed in Anglesey, when we both played in a mixed hockey match. My friend, with whom I always shared accommodation, was from Croydon, she met and married an Irishman and moved to Dublin where she still lives, Mrs. Margaret C. Another friend from Hertford, is now living in Merseyside. I am still in contact with them and others.

Regarding a query about brides married in Colwyn Bay in those years not disclosing their occupation in the marriage records, at that time married women were not allowed to work for any civil service, so many anxious to prevent disclosure at risk of losing their jobs. Of course like most young people in wartime we 'lost' our teenage years as such. The day we heard we were to be returned to London, I don't think there was a dry eye either on the train or the friends waving us off. My husband and I went back often in later years to see friends in the Bay with our children. Others have remained very close, only infirmities now keep us apart. My son took me to stay with Mr and Mrs Roberts in 2007.

One thing that caused a certain resentment was when the celebrations on the TV for the 60th anniversary of the war covered the servicemen, firefighters, nurses, ambulance people, Home Guard, merchant services and with a little nudge, the Land Army. Nowhere was there a mention of the thousands of civil servants sent to so many locations to serve their country and who also lost the chance to do a degree course.

The whole object of the enormous task was to ensure safe working on and compilation of ration books. This was a huge task as Great Britain could not supply all the dietary needs. Lend-Lease was founded and tremendous statistical work was involved via the three countries the UK the USA and Canada. A lengthy process. We were headed at top level by Professor Drummond, a brilliant man who, with his family, was murdered while on a camping holiday in France, well after the war.[151] Many well known scientific, technical and medical people were involved. I worked for Alice Barter.

After a couple of years the Stationery Office issued 'The Food Consumption Levels Enquiry'. Listing every dietary need, vitamins, etc. There were a few copies issued, I still have mine. Every day memos came round inviting us to change course, cipher interpreters, etc. Mrs Roberts and I applied for all, just to get more interesting work, but to no avail. One day a memo came inviting applicants for a nine-month course on statistics as there was an overall shortage of statisticians in the government. They wanted four applicants from each Ministry. We applied at once, along with others, interviews and tests followed, and we were both successful. We were off to the London School of Economics, seconded to a college in Jesus Lane, Cambridge. We were in different lodgings, but went to daily lectures. It was fascinating work, with exams at the end. Fortunately both Mrs Roberts and I were successful and returned to Colwyn Bay as statisticians under different bosses. Life was infinitely more interesting.

Most of the Ministries returned to London in the autumn of 1944. I continued to work for the Statistics and Intelligence Departments in Stanmore until 1947, when having married in 1945, I was expecting twins.

*Olwen Hughes (née Dodd)*
Olwen was a clerical officer in the Ministry from 1940 to 1946. Her home was in Old Colwyn at the time. She had left school at fourteen for financial reasons, her father was sick and there were younger children in the family. She was persuaded to leave her laundry job to join the Ministry by two civil-servant lodgers from London. She felt some local businesses suffered from loss of staff when the Ministry arrived, but they would not employ her until after she had handed in her notice. She felt lucky to have been chosen to go to the London School of Economics on a statistics course at Jesus College, Cambridge, and completed a one-year course in just a few months. She said she would always be grateful to the Ministry for that. Her division was the Canned and Dried Milk Department, first in the Rothsay on the promenade, then in the Pwllycrochan Hotel. She remembers many of the men clerks being in the Home Guard.

Women's lives surely changed since their previous employment would have been staffing hotels, restaurants and cafes. Many were introduced to a clerical life. But her mother did not take up employment as she had three children under eight-years old. She found this frustrating as she had previously been a German translator and had come from London and would love to have joined the Ministry. Every hotel or other Ministry venue had to have a firewatch team, the Pwllycrochan Hotel had six in their team. Her clerical job was the recording of Merchant Navy ships carrying Lend-Lease stocks of dried milk and recording their transfer to buffer depots all over Britain. She and her colleagues saw Lord Woolton often because he always dined in the Pwllycrochan Hotel canteen, supposedly the best of all the hotels that were taken over. She remembers the social activity, cinemas, plenty of dancing (more so when other foreign regiments were billeted there). Sunday nights at the Odeon and the Repertory Theatre involved mainly classical shows, although there were famous dance bands at the former. Now she is Olwen Hughes, and left the area to be near family only in 2007.[152]

*Elizabeth*
Elizabeth left Llanrwst Grammar School in June 1940 having gained her GCE Certificate, which is all she would have needed to enter the Normal teacher-training college in Bangor on her eighteenth birthday, which was

eighteen months away. She applied for a junior job at the Ministry of Food and found herself a junior clerical assistant at Penrhos College, adapted as a 'Bacon and Ham' checking centre amidst a host of well-qualified civil servants. She was paid £4 10s per week for checking forms of in-take and out-take of large firms like Palethorps and Baxters. All these in pink print.

They were known locally as 'Guinea Pigs' because they were housed in various boarding houses where they contributed a guinea (21 shillings) a week for a bed, with two or three of them sharing a bedroom and having a very basic breakfast. The rest of the day they had to feed themselves in the canteen where they were working. It was very simple, plain food but they survived on it, plus the air was beneficial breathing while walking from the guinea residence to Penrhos College. After a couple of months of existing like this, she returned home, deciding to try to become a student teacher at a couple of schools that were willing to include her as a helper in preparation for her teaching career. The tedium of the monotonous daily checking could have been very soul destroying and she considered herself very lucky to be able to pursue her teaching career.

*Audrey Andrew – one of the influx*
Audrey was told by a friend about the letter in the magazine and wrote to me. I later phoned her. It seemed she made a lifelong career out of her early work as a civil servant. After leaving school and attending a secretarial college in Liverpool she passed the civil-service exams and was accepted for a job in London in August 1939 at the Board of Trade Food Defence Plans, which soon became the Ministry of Food. From there she was evacuated and was among the influx of the 5,000 that arrived in Colwyn Bay on trains within a few days of each other. We talked of her experiences, and she remembered many of the departments and various buildings. Her work was within the Milk Department of the Ministry of Food in Norfolk House, working with statistics. She told me her friend Margaret had a very important job, and accompanied her boss, Mr Bradley, to Canada to conferences. Bravely, Audrey exchanged jobs with another clerical officer in January 1942 to be nearer her family in Liverpool, then in 1943 she joined the Auxilliary Territorial Service[153] and moved back again to London. She was demobbed in September 1946 and came back to Colwyn Bay to work in Establishment in the Colwyn Bay Hotel until 1947, when she joined the

Liverpool Food Office. Surprisingly, she tells me it was based in the Walker Art Gallery, and later relocated to Hughes' department store. She says she has rarely worked in purpose-built offices, they were always church halls or other buildings. Then, after various Food Office moves, she joined the Inland Revenue in Birkenhead and was promoted to inspector of taxes and worked in the tax office in Colwyn Bay. She worked locally until she was fifty when she retired. She is now 88.

Staff were still traveling south even up until 1946. E.B. wrote from Essex.

In the Summer of 1946 I was nineteen and had been working for the Ministry of Food Egg Division for several years when a notice came round asking for volunteers to go to Colwyn Bay for a month, work in the Establishment department, then return to London with them – replacing staff who wanted to stay in Colwyn Bay. I volunteered with Phyllis, a girl of my age, Bill, a chap a bit older that us, and Mr Thompson, an old chap. When we arrived, the others went to Establishment but I was sent to Canned Fish Department to work for the assistant director and his deputy as they wanted to return to London – the rest of the department stayed in Colwyn Bay. Bill had been there before so was able to show Phyllis and me around and we had a good time. I thought it was a great place, but have never been back.

## 8: The War

I borrowed the diary of Captain S. H. Cutler, MC, TD, 61st Medium Regiment, Royal Artillery. The diary runs from 30 June 1944 to 3 December 1945 and it was lent to me by Vicky Cutler. I was so amazed that she was prepared to lend a stranger this fascinating document that belonged to her father. I had written a request to her, and also told her how I found out it existed, and how I empathized with the irreplaceable value this has to her. When I read the diary it reaffirmed why she would be so proud. The initials TD after Military Cross means Territorial Decoration.

> Wednesday, 7 February. Letter from home to say that I have been awarded the MC. This is the first I heard of it. Mother saw it in the times.
>
> 10 February. My MC announced today by CAGRA – he has been awarded the DSO.

The diary is a factual account of the movements of the 61st Medium Regiment providing a timeline of the war, with information about casualties. It is very unemotional, which is what the soldiers would have to be to function and survive. Some of the written information may not have been discussed back home. Leave was written in from 17–28 Feb 1945, and he says,

> Heaviest bomber raids of the war on Germany. New American push with all USA armies Canadians and 2nd Army attack doing well. Russians advancing. Turkey and Egypt declare war on Germany and Japan.

I met Captain Harry Parker Royal Artillery, who was recommended as a contributor by a friend. I had attended school with his son, Harry himself attended Colwyn Bay Grammar School, known then as the County School, and joined the Territorial Army in 1939. He says,

In August I was called up with the Denbighshire Yeomanry, 61st Medium Regiment (with Captain Cutler). Demobbed in July 1946. Most of the local men joined the Territorial Army battery in 1939, there was one in Wrexham and one in Llanrwst.

Harry said there is a book published called *The Freedom of the Burghers*, detailing an honour which was bestowed on the 61st Medium and in the book are all the names of all the men in the Territorial Army who were called up. There were Ray and Sid, the two brothers of Captain Cutler. H.P. goes on to say,

> I was a Surveyor and Quartermaster. I was too busy to write diaries during the war. They taught me how to survey. After Dunkirk we formed new units, went to Hull and Yorkshire and was posted, that is where I met my wife. And it became a training regiment. Then we went to the Middle East, Italy, South of France, Marseilles, Germany and was involved in the surrender of Dunkirk. Stayed away the whole time no leave to return home. I was not here during the wartime years. I did have some leave in 1940 and 1941 before I was posted abroad.

A local hero remembered by schoolboys of the day was Air Marshal Sir Denis Crowley Milling, KCB, CBE, DSO, DFC & Bar, AE, an RAF ace. He was a distinguished fighter pilot in the Battle of Britain.

The tanks going through the town from Trawsfynedd or Anglesey to Liverpool wrecked the roads and pavements. The soldiers who would have been in the town and at Kinmel Camp would have been the Pioneer Corps, Royal Signals, Royal Artillery. They were manning guns. The park in Rhos was labelled 'The Gunny' and was really heaven for young boys to watch the military activity. There were convoys from Bryn Euryn, ships and aircraft came in and there was a station on Bryn Euryn with a cable leading up the steep bank to the hut on the top.[154] The station on the summit of Bryn Euryn was for direction finding. If a plane did not know where it was, the navigator could get a fix from this and at least one other to locate himself precisely.[155]

D.R. & D.R. said:

> We had all these soldiers billeted around and YMCA in the church hall across here. Methodist church hall and Rhos United Reform Church hall

too [now awaiting demolition]. We lived on Elwy Road in those days about five doors down from Brompton Lodge – there is an entry for a garage where the soldiers used to come and do their exercises. Sergeants were a real horror. The area was a training ground, guns in the park. They had two houses opposite the squash club, I was in the Girls Training Corps then. We had to put our gas masks on and the sergeant made us take our gas masks off and the tears were running. He thought we were a lot of kids in early teens. Those houses are still empty now [since been demolished]. They have never gone well. The people who owned them would have had to be paid. It did make people do things together suddenly in wartime people work together. People invited soldiers to have baths in their houses.

Most of the local people in Colwyn Bay had never experienced anything serious. There were very few stray bombs here. The author remembers seeing bomb sites in the 1950s when as a child her parents drove though Liverpool. There was so much damage it was horrific.

D.B. says,

> On the pier, there was an exercise to prevent invasion – they took planks out of both piers.' On the rugby field they put up poles to stop gliders landing. There was a Spitfire crashed by Rhos laundry.

But H.F. says,

> We did alright, not too much hardship, no bombing but the German planes would come up the coast of Ireland and see the lights of Belfast then make a beeline across. Shrewsbury got the first warning then they set the alarm off her, usually between seven and nine and in the evening. We would go to a room in the house. We could see the burning of Liverpool across the sea. Bombers would jettison bombs on their return via this route.

J.L. says,

> We only had about three bombs the whole time. Well we could see the bombs burning in Liverpool. The only time we had bombs was when they were flying away from Manchester and Liverpool where they had been bombing and they would be dropping them and ours would be chasing them and they would be dogfights over Elwy Road fields. There was once when I was in guides in that church hall on Elwy Road and the siren went and the silly old woman who was in charge sent us home you see well I

was running across the fields and there was 'Dudududududu' in the sky there was fighting above. No air raid shelters, not here. The only bombs I remember were in Dinerth Road about three fell and we had the sea mines and the tanks going through Colwyn Bay they made marks all over the road.[156]

But the only bomb we know of fell in Dinerth Road Fields. My mother heard it. She went out each time there was a siren. She would not go in the shelter, and another time she saw a Spitfire doing a victory roll after bringing down a plane over Denbigh. There was a landmine in Llandulas duck pond with a terrific explosion. There had been a lot of opposition to this pond, well it was demolished then. And there were sea mines which came across in rough weather and when they washed up against the shore they exploded loudly. During the blackout there were no streetlights. We used to put a strip on a torch or a bicycle light with a chink of light coming out.[157]

# 9: Developments and Impact

G.T.: Our world was widened because it was a new culture that came in, It was a tremendous influx so that every available space was taken up by people.[158]

P.B.: I saw no difference in the social life, coming from the Wirral.[159]

As Britain's experience of war was said by Marwick to be set apart from that of Europe by its degree of effect,[160] in a similar way North Wales was set apart from Liverpool and other cities. For example 60,000 civilians were killed in Britain, but North Wales was relatively unscathed and untargeted. Many contributors had witnessed the bombing of Merseyside from the coast, watching the sky redden with fire during raids, and were always vigilant for bombs jettisoned by returning planes, one experiencing a dogfight overhead near her house,[161] therefore danger was a reality. There were famously 'Few' nationally to whom so many owed so much, but *all* played their part and without concerted effort success could not have been achieved. Effects on the area, which were lasting, were the hosting of fleeing populations and a necessity in continuing to absorb the Merseyside population up until the present day.

A huge evacuee intake meant that education had to be reorganised in both private and state schools; *A Welcome in the Hillside?*[162] documents the impact and evidence is supported by J.L. and G.T. and others. Editorials and letters published in the *North Wales Weekly News* give a valuable insight into how the populace reacted. There was particular antipathy reported regarding the Merseyside evacuees, reinforced by evidence of the oral history contributors. It was said in the press that Welsh social and cultural life was undermined, not only in language but also in manners, habits, religion and the whole routine of domestic life.[163] There was naturally an effect of wartime on the people culturally and economically, which was particular to this area.

Some Welsh Nationalists caused concern by their extreme reluctance to enlist, arguing that they would be fighting for England and not for Wales. Plaid Cymru had declared neutrality at the outbreak of war.[164] Welsh language and culture has historically been separate during the gradual and extensive influx of English migrants. Plaid Cymru was formally established in 1925 to defend the Welsh language and culture. It is clear that the English input has been substantial in the development of the coastal areas in the nineteenth and twentieth centuries. There is little recognition of the considerable contribution the area made during the war in its capacity to shelter people and in particular departments of wartime function. However, it has been argued that the disruption of the family was the most traumatic factor for children living under air raid conditions, and evacuation was said to reveal the deep social division within British society.[165] It brought a consciousness of deplorable conditions prevalent in Britain's industrial cities, and so raised awareness. Evidence of this has been shown repeatedly in original oral histories of the town. Welsh culture and language was threatened with dilution. The classes mixed out of necessity, as they also did in the shelter of the tube stations in London.

> There are many personal records of friendliness and social contact, which seem to transcend normal social barriers. But in part this can be explained by a need, in time of danger to communicate freely and avoid conditions of social isolation.[166]

The mixed population rich and poor shared what they had gladly; they supported the new influx, some feeling inferior to the sophisticates of London and the civil service. They gained new insights in days before travel or media.

> There were some very nice people but then there were others. Our world was widened because it was a new culture that came in, a new way of looking at things and doing things which had been foreign to us before. It was a tremendous influx so that every available space was taken up by people. They expected to go out every night, whereas I came from a culture where you only went out on a Friday or Saturday night. There could be some spats between people At a concert one of the others chose to sing the very song that she was going to sing! It was lovely for all us children to see, the dramas.[167]

G.T. maintains that Colwyn Bay grew and changed, ameliorated in some cases.

> There were things that arrived here that would never have if it wasn't for the war. We had a lot of new different shops here, theatres, cinemas were always full, you could go to a different cinema four nights a week or every night one or two were like fleapits but that wasn't the point there was still a big queue to get in. There used to be big concerts at the pier and there used to be summer season of shows. There were cinemas like the Cosy. Sybil Thorndike came to the Pier Pavilion. She came to the speech day at school. There were also the Squadronaires an Air Force band at the Odeon. There was an open-air dance in Eirias Park to celebrate the end of the war.[168]

The Ministry of Food had a hundred members in a choir. Many editorials over the war years in the *North Wales Weekly News* illustrate this. P.R. was a performer at the theatre and she remembers many talented actors and actresses in the wartime concerts. Not all of the influx were poor. The local paper almost every week throughout the war showed adverts for furs. G.T. explains:

> I am not sure if you could get a fur coat without coupons [indeed, furs were not rationed]. Of course, there were a lot of very rich people living in Colwyn Bay before the war, big houses, and as they died off, their fur coats could be remodelled.[169]

In the summer of 1938 it was said that 150,000 people fled to Welsh hotels 'to sit out he war drinking gin, reading novels and playing cards.'[170]

By 1944, 48% of all civil-service employees were women.[171] P.B., O.R. and G.T. have discussed their work with the Ministry. Women changed their employment patterns, housewives now working alongside single women and the standard of living in working-class households rose. Horizons had been widened by the experience of working with and socialising with women from cities such as Merseyside, Manchester and London, and of the mixing of the working and middle classes. Women found employment in munitions factories, assembling military vehicles and as clerks in the Ministry of Food, and others in support work, as in landladies and carers of evacuees. Twenty-two percent of employed workers in Wales were said

*Colwyn Bay Pier, photographed in the 1920s. [W. Alister Williams Collection]*

to be in the armed forces by 1944 and a further 33% engaged in civilian work associated with the war. Unemployment had all but disappeared. Some 100,000 people had left Wales for England. Unemployment in Wales decreased overall as a result of the war,[172] particularly in the Colwyn Bay area. Light industry was further established after the war years to counteract the decline of the tourist trade

There were demographic changes in the subsequent decades, but not an increase in population. In 1931, the population of the municiple borough was 20,886, increasing to 22,283 in 1951,[173] but it was a population of a different and changed character. Wartime marriages had caused spouses to relocate. A continuous influx from England has been maintained as tourism failed in later decades. Gaps then became filled with the unemployed moving into houses of multiple occupation, which, as predicted, is a major cause of local concern.

> We still have influx coming in from Liverpool. While there was work on the slum clearance after the war, the Liverpool [poverty] would spread throughout Deeside and the North Wales coast to Prestatyn, Rhyl and right across the coast.[174]

The issues beg comparison to other seaside resorts in decline that are now experiencing regeneration. But a town so small was seriously and permanently disrupted, with 38 buildings requisitioned, hotels along with schools, with serious effect. Many of the hotels remained empty or became government offices e.g. the Metropole which was the Department of Administrative Finance, where P.B. and B.D. worked, during and after the war. Some years ago it was converted into flats. Some hotels were converted into convalescent or retirement homes, others were demolished and replaced by apartments, particularly for the retired, who it is said hardly enliven the town. There were fewer boarding houses than there had been before the war.

There is virtually no recognition of the considerable wartime contribution made by Colwyn Bay, since events of the day went undocumented and are virtually unknown and unmentioned among the current population. The Earl of Woolton did not acknowledge the town or population in his memoir, but did acknowledge the lack of documentation of the work. The designer and overseer of the construction of Mulberry harbour was unacknowledged for decades and received small financial reward and no recognition until recent years. Nearby Gwrych Castle secretly housed a nuber of German Jewish children until the creation of the state of Israel. Further afield, Manod Quarry was not returned to the owners until the 1980s, to the detriment of the quarrying industry.

P.B. commented on the scarcity of houses in wartime, and it can be verified by the large number of 'Houses Wanted' notices in the press. While B.D. had said that in 1938, when her father relocated his family, there had been in excess of 500 houses available to rent. This shortage increased further with the return of the military to civilian life. By 1948, there were 1,000 families waiting for council housing. There were government restrictions due to the widespread shortages of materials and the focus was on areas harder hit. The result was a huge building programme eventually taking place and four council estates were built over the next decades. Colwyn Bay had not suffered bombing, but its sea defences had caused the promenade, one of its greatest positive features, to suffer neglect, which was detrimental to the holiday trade, the main opportunity for the recovery of its economy. The great population influx of the war years had a huge impact in that it has been widely believed to contribute to the deconstruction of the tourist industry. In a balanced view, other facts must be considered, as with the current trend all seaside areas have suffered decline, the nature of travel having changed since the 1950s. The eventual building of an expressway, planned in the 1960s, cut a swathe straight through the Colwyn Bay town centre which also had a negative and lasting impact.

Attempts have been made to counteract the effects of a destroyed economy. As a measure to boost tourism after the war, Colwyn Bay successfully hosted an event which was beneficial. The 1947 *Eisteddfodd*, a traditional festival of music, was so highly successful with an attendance of 150,000, that huge profits were used to pay for amenities such as a Welsh-medium school (established in a private house in the town in 1950) and a Welsh reference room in the library. Colwyn Bay once again had succumbed to a huge influx of people, but this time a typically Welsh event, despite the fact that the population of 21,000 was at that time only one-third Welsh, as if to compensate for the alleged wartime dilution of culture. Similarly, the celebrations for the coronation of Queen Elizabeth II in 1953 brought a huge influx of visitors albeit on a very temporary basis.[175]

The civil service population had left gradually as testified by P.B., when for example the department 'Bacon and Ham' went to Stanmore in 1943. Amongst those who left were local people, like P.B. and P.R. and A.R, relocating with new career prospects. By the end of the war, the cultural input and patronage the Ministry of Food had made to all the cinemas and theatres, art and dramatic societies had diminished drastically, pre-empting the demise of the seaside-entertainment business. Efforts were made, but not even the film festival devised by the newly formed Chamber of Trade in 1948 could offset the decline.[176] D.B. and B.W. commented:

> There was a good football team in the town. Some of the Ministry of Food were members. It continued to be a good team after the Ministry left.[177]

> The Cricket Club had some charity matches, I played as a 12-year old in 1944. There were matches during the war. There were locals and outside teams.[178]

Those matches raised incredible sums of money, as stated in chapter 4.

Fortunately, the popularity of cricket, rugby and football did not

*Interior Cartmell Hotel, Station Road (now the Prince Madoc), from an Edwardian postcard.*

deteriorate as testified by B.W. and Mellor, in *A Club History*,[179] but thrived with the return home of the military service personnel after 1945. By 1955, the allotments at Eirias Park had been converted into a large sports arena. What had been the Toc H canteen, where A.D.'s mother had worked at catering for the military, and running church functions during the war, became the Friendship Club, run by the Borough Youth Council very successfully with a membership which grew in only two years to 200 plus. By 1952, it had 370 members effectively promoting citizenship.[180] This had resulted from a wartime endeavour and maintained a climate of camaraderie, which as above has been said to exist in wartime.

'In June 1944 the Mayor and Mayoress (Councillor and Mrs A. E. Neill) entertained to dinner at Cartmells' Hotel in Station Road, the servicemen with their wives, who had been repatriated from prisoner-of-war camps in Europe.'[181] The author's godparents would have been present.

## 10: 'Opportunity or Menace?'[182]
## Does the town now deserve credit and reparation?

*'The town was transformed and energised by the war.'*
An amazing social life with entertainment and retail opportunities ensued with the coming of outside influences in an age before the media became all pervasive. The area gained advantages in return for the disruption experienced. It was 'heaven for young boys' said D.B., 'with the arrival of soldiers, planes and military exercises'.[183] North Wales was ideal for the purpose of hosting and hiding – sparsely populated, with plentiful accommodation. Secrets were safe, despite the inquisitive nature of the Welsh people. MI5 double agents remained undiscovered, ensconced in North Wales hotels; the building of the Mulberry Harbour was a secret from even some who were building it; the shelter of the Jewish refugees at Gwrych is still almost unknown. The antagonism of the nationalists did not cause undue problems. Although there was antipathy towards the Merseyside evacuees, kindness, personal sacrifices and duty to individuals eclipsed concern for the dilution of the culture and economic hardship. The lack of acknowledgement and appreciation for the degree to which the town of Colwyn Bay was inconvenienced was naturally perceived as insignificant while serious casualties and devastation occurred in other areas. There may have been a possibility of further use of the town during the political crises of the 1950s.

It has been disclosed in recent oral evidence that the area benefited greatly in some ways, being 'enlivened'. The distance from London and the inconveniences suffered by the incoming staff of the Ministry did not affect their performance and they succeeded against all odds in this valuable contribution, locals and influx working together so that the lack of food nationally did not lead to loss of morale. Former civil servants have pointed out the lack of recognition given for their success in an important role of the organisation of feeding the nation, where all other tasks were given credit.[184] North Wales had a unique experience of war, more remote, but did not suffer as in comparison to other areas. Liverpool was bombed, sadly with heavy losses, but such cities have now been thoroughly regenerated while Colwyn Bay has deteriorated through loss of its own industry. It must be time to acknowledge, credit, repay and invest in the town's future. The Welsh Assembly offices were built during the war years for additional office space. Decanting departments worked well in wartime, to repeat this in the twenty-first century may be ecological by helping to diffuse populations from congested areas, although even if planned, this may take generations to evolve.

One of the contributors maintains that as far as this area is concerned there is a sub strata of people, and outsiders are still coming in. People who went to school here have a bond, but retired people relocating here will never integrate, as they have nothing in common. 'I became a teacher here after the war and about 3,000 boys know me. They open doors for me now and are pleased to see me.'[185]

Without an inclusion to the local network, oral history would have been unachievable and lack of documentation would make this study unworkable.

To return to the specific questions asked.

What was the contribution of the area to the war effort? —

Safety, shelter, secrecy, a certain amount of industry as in other towns, but there were also particular contributions such as diamond tool manufacture and essential administrative support to the Ministry in the feeding of the nation.

What was the impact of the war on this area? —

There was serious disruption by an influx of population, reorganisation of education, but the additional employment available was welcomed. The area was greatly enlivened socially, culturally and sportively. Marriage to partners from outside areas occurred as it also did in other towns and this is worthy of further research. Social mixing and awareness of deprivation was observed in some areas and in other cases a new degree of sophistication encountered and welcomed.

How did the area change because of the war?—

Tourism was destroyed by requisitioning before the advent of foreign travel, because when the influx left, the town was deflated and depleted. Some believe that war was the demise of tourism in Colwyn Bay. Women's lives had changed as they had all over the country. Welsh culture was said to be diluted, but this was compensated somewhat by the results produced by the efforts of the *Eisteddfod* which funded the Welsh-medium school and Welsh room in the library. Full regeneration is now overdue and is gradually beginning with a 'Bay Life Initiative.'

Was the contribution recognised? —

The Earl of Woolton did not mention the town in his memoir in the 1950s, and neither does the obituary of John Raeburn in the *Times* and the *Telegraph* in 2006. The exhibition at the Imperial War Museum does not mention that the headquarters of the Ministry of Food was in Colwyn Bay. There is very little awareness. Further afield, Manod Quarry was not returned to the owner until the 1980s, the design and building of Mulberry Harbours went unrecognised for decades. The Jewish refugee children, now elderly, have formed a society with a website and their presence during wartime is now becoming known. The Mountain Rescue service was recognised with the founder being awarded an MBE. Some executives were eventually given honours for their work with the Ministry of Food, for example Alec Parselle (but not until 1954), Mr Ebert an MBE and Jack Drummond a knighthood. Clerical workers from the Ministry do not seek or expect any credit, but felt they had a benefit in gaining employment, in contributing and in envisaging new horizons. Time has elapsed so that a new perspective on the war years can be viewed, but the rich oral evidence, of which only a fragment has been collected and recorded will no longer be available within the foreseeable future.

# Notes

### Introduction
1. Ivor Wynne Jones and Norman Tucker, *Colwyn Bay Its History Through the Years*, Landmark, UK, 1995, p.225.
2. G. Edwards, *The Borough of Colwyn Bay. A Social History, 1934–1974*, 1984, p.37.
3. Informed by the National Archives that civil service records have been destroyed.
4. Stephen Caunce, *Oral History and the Local Historian*, Longman, London, 1994, p.129.
5. J. Tosh, Pursuit of History, Longman, London, 2002, p.193.

### 1: Food plans under the flightpath
6. *Land at War 1939–1944*, HMSO, 1945, quoted in Reg Chambers Jones', *Bless 'Em All: Aspects of the War in North-West Wales, 1939–45*, Bridge Books, Wrexham, 1995, p.50.
7. As in Eire and Scotland too.
8. Unknown to him 'Ladymay', an Austrian woman was feeding information as a double agent.
9. http://www.subbrit.org.uk/rsg/features/government.
10. Ivor Wynne Jones and Norman Tucker, *Colwyn Bay. Its History Across the Years*, p.226.
11. *The Independent*, 15 January 2010.
12. A. M. Low, *Benefits of War*, 1943, cited in A. Marwick, *War and Social Change in the Twentieth Century*, Hampshire, Macmillan, 1974, .p.151.

### 2: The wider area of North Wales. Safety, secrets and spies.
13. National Archives, MAF 72/58.
14. There are many articles in the local press relating to the degree of welcome extended in Colwyn Bay. The Council of Social Service Minutes, 8 February 1940, DRO DD/DM/121/1, states there is 'plenty of poverty in Colwyn Bay without being saddled with the responsibilities of providing for Liverpool children.
15. Operation Kindertransport. Details from the website http://www.gwrychtrust.co.uk/html/operation_kindertransport..
16. Reg Chambers Jones', *Bless 'Em All: Aspects of the War in North-West Wales, 1939–45*, Bridge Books, Wrexham, 1995, p.23.
17. Reg Chambers Jones', *Bless 'Em All: Aspects of the War in North-West Wales, 1939–45*, Bridge Books, Wrexham, 1995, p.24.
18. G.T. resident in interview on 21 April 2007.
19. Rhydymwyn Storage Site. Details from the website http://www.rvsweb.org.uk/ourhistory.htm#AShortHistory 10 April 2007. At the end of 1938 the Government decided that the question of storing large quantities of Pyro and Runcol (Mustard Gas) in bulk

with complete protection from bombs should be considered and ICI was asked to submit proposals for dealing with a capacity of 1,500 tons. This was in addition to the general requirements for safe storage.
20. M Hughes, Conwy Mulberry Harbour, Gwasg Carreg Gwalch, Llanrwst, 2001.
21. I. Wynne Jones, Hitler's Celtic Echo, Pegasus, Llandudno, 2006, chapter 2. The Welsh Suspect List..
22. O.R. interview April 2007.
23. I. Wynne Jones, Hitler's Celtic Echo, Pegasus, Llandudno, 2006, p.18.
24. North Wales Weekly News, 15 February 1940.
25. I. Wynne Jones, Hitler's Celtic Echo, Pegasus, Llandudno, 2006, p.31.
26. I. Wynne Jones, Hitler's Celtic Echo, Pegasus, Llandudno, 2006, p.77.
27. HO 45/25572 at the National Archives, closed until 2005.
28. J.L. interview on 18 April 2007.
29. I. Wynne Jones, Hitler's Celtic Echo, Pegasus, Llandudno, 2006, p.164.
30. The National Archives, NA PRO KV 4/211 in I. Wynne Jones, Hitler's Celtic Echo, Pegasus, Llandudno, 2006, p.183–8.
31. Wikipaedia.

## 3: Colwyn Bay and its particular contribution. 'The town was transformed and energised by the war.'
32. D.B. oral history contributor.
33. Braid's papers at Denbighshire Record Office, DD/MM/1176/1.
34. A. and F.D. interview, 13 April 2007.
35. Braid's papers, DRO DD/MM/1176/1 and the evidence of Mr F. Davies.
36. Evidence from Hans Wins, son of the factory founder.
37. Author's experience.
38. Conversations with Hans Wins.
39. Lieutenant-Colonel J. R. Williams, An Autobiography, Gee & Son,Ltd., Denbigh, 1961.
40. Information from Mr F. Davies.
41. O.R. interview, April 2007.
42. Henry Smith, Bureaucrats in Battledress, A History of the Ministry of Food Home Guard, Conwy, 1945.
43. www.manchester.ac.uk/history/research/cchw/research/contestinghomedefence.
44. Henry Smith, Bureaucrats in Battledress, A History of the Ministry of Food Home Guard, p.122–4 in P. Summerfield & C. Peniston–Bird, Contesting Home Defence, Manchester University Press. Manchester. 2007.

## 4: The Ministry of Food: 'Food town on sea'
45. North Wales Weekly News, 16 January 1941.
46. North Wales Weekly News, 3 April 1941.
47. G. E. Mellor, Colwyn Bay Cricket Club – A Club History, Rhos Press, 1992.
48. North Wales Weekly News, 20 September 1945, p.7.
49. G. E. Mellor, Colwyn Bay Cricket Club – A Club History, Rhos Press, 1992.
50. North Wales Weekly News, 8 May 1941.
51. All documents of the first Ministry of Food from the first war, retained by the Board of

Trade Food Department after 1918, were deposited in the Ministry of Pensions archives. They were then subjected to periodic weeding and destruction under Public Record Office Schedule until 1937, when further destruction was halted at the request of the Board of Trade. The papers were subsequently removed in lots for examination. No further destruction took place and the remaining documents were eventually lodged with the second Ministry of Food archives.

52. *Memoirs of the Rt Hon Earl of Woolton*, Cassel, London, 1959, p.186, chapter entitled 'The Businessman in Government'.
53. National Archives, MAF 102/60.
54. ibid.
55. *Memoirs of the Rt Hon Earl of Woolton*, Cassel, London, 1959, p.179.
56. ibid, p.207.
57. ibid, p.189.
58. ibid, p.203.
59. Staff at the National Archives say some civil service records were destroyed.
60. Population was 21,000 in 1931 rising to only 24,500 in 2004. Colwyn Bay is the second largest conurbation in North Wales. http://www.conwy.gov.uk/E_MINTES/e_post2002/e_scrutiny/e_economic/e_reports/07-colwyn_bay_regen-fund_Bid.pdf, April 12 2007.
61. *Memoirs of the Rt Hon Earl of Woolton*, Cassel, London, 1959, p.184
62. *North Wales Weekly News*, 10 April 1941.
63. *North Wales Weekly News*, 4 February 1943.
64. *Daily Telegraph*, 22 July 2006.
65. Requisitioning orders marked 'Secret'. Denbighshire Record Office, DD/PO/481.
66. Agents emergency work. Marked 'Secret'. Denbishshire Record Office, DRO DD/PO/481.
67. Albert Rigby private papers, Imperial War Museum 94/6/1.
68. Relocation to Colwyn Bay, the National Archives, MAF 83/945.
69. ibid.
70. ibid.
71. Priority phone calls, the National Archives, MAF 83/945.
72. Ivor Wynne Jones and Norman Tucker, *Colwyn Bay. Its History Across the Years*, p.227.
73. Letter from Lord Woolton, the National Archives, MAF 83/945
74. Unanimous evidence of all contributors who had worked at the Ministry.
75. To Sir Quentin Hill, 14 August 1940, the National Archives, MAF 102/55.
76. *Memoirs of the Rt Hon Earl of Woolton*, Cassel, London, 1959, p.250.
77. Letter from Robert Westerby held by the National Archives, MAF 102/55.
78. ibid.
79. Albert Rigby private papers.94/6/1 at Imperial War Museum.
80. Mr A. Ebert. 76/68/1 at Imperial War Museum.

## 5: Social, cultural and economic effects of the influx

81. Ministry of Information speaker, Mrs L Hayward, Colwyn Bay Pier, reported in the *North Wales Weekly News*, 27 March 27 1941.
82. Advertisment in the *North Wales Weekly News*, 21 January 1943.
83. http://www.aim25.ac.uk/cgi-bin/vcdf/detail?coll_id=5768&inst_id=1&nv1=search&nv2=
84. Henry Smith, *Bureaucrats in Battledress, A History of the Ministry of Food Home Guard*, Conwy, 1945.

85. P. Summerfield and C. Peniston Bird, *Contesting Home Defence*, Manchester, Manchester University Press, 2007 p.67.
86. Parish records of St Paul's and St John's 1939–48 held at Colwyn Bay Library.
87. We assess how many local women or men married someone from area 4. and vice versa. It is not the case that we wish to monitor intermarriage between the English and the Welsh, as the delineation is questionable, would that be born in Wales? Father Welsh? Or Welsh spoken? Colwyn Bay is rather anglicised and always has been. Cheshire and Liverpool are geographically nearer than South Wales, which has very poor transport links. North and South Wales are distant in both geography and affiliation.
88. Mrs J. Wooley.
89. A.W. interviews.
90. Captain Harry Parker, RA, retired schoolmaster at Pendorlan and Eirias High Schools.
91. G.T. interview, 12 April 2007.
92. ibid.

**6: Oral History. Reflections. Evidence of the former population**

93. Albert Rigby, many conversations and letters.
94. J. Wallis, *A Welcome in the Hillside?*, Avid, Wirral, 2000.
95. Colwyn Bay Council of Social Service Minutes 8 February 1940. DD/DM/121/1 quoted in J. Wallis, *A Welcome in the Hillside?*, p.111.
96. Interview with J.L., 18 April 2010.
97. *North Wales Weekly News,* 14 March 1940, 'There is alarm at the monoglot English children, plans to give instruction in Welsh. Financial and cultural loss to Wales'.
98. *North Wales Weekly News,* 23 May 1940, 'A Welshman's Fears'.
99. *North Wales Weekly News,* Public Notices, 27 June 1940.
100. Interview with D. and D.R., 20 June 2007.
101. B. Whale, former principal of the Wireless College. Telephone interview, 22 June 2007.
102. P.B. received a medal for her services to WVS, but told me that she had not expected it and just wanted to do the work. She is now 98.
103. H.F. interview, 22 June 2007.
104. Albert Rigby, 25 June 2007.
105. Evidence of Dr John Wainwright, Deganwy, 2009.
106. Monica Beardsworth, *Penrhos College 1880–1980, the second fifty years*, Bristol.
107. G.T. interview, 12 April 2007.
108. D.B. interview, 19 April 2007
109. A.W. interviewed on numerous occasions.
110. G.T. interview, 12 April 2007.
111. B.W. interview, 19 April 2007.
112. *North Wales Weekly News*, 7 January 1940, 'There is alarm at the monoglot English children, plans to give instruction in Welsh. Financial and cultural loss to Wales'.
113. Apparently these huts were built during the First World War.
114. G.T. interview, 12 April 2007.
115. B.W. interview, 19 April 2007.
116. Great-grandmother and grandmother Beryl of author's son, who provided the impetus for this book.
117. J.B. interview, 21 April 2007.

118. H.F. interview, 22 June 2007.
119. B.W. interview, 19 April 2007.
120. G. E. Mellor, *Colwyn Bay Cricket Club. A Club History*, Rhos Press, 1992, p.13.
121. H.W. interviewed on numerous occasions.
122. Ivor Wynne Jones, *Hitler's Celtic Echo*, Pegasus, Llandudno, 2006, p.81.
123. Derek Bellis interview, 19 April 2007.
124. Albert Rigby many interviews and conversations, 2007–9.
125. G.T. interview, 12 April 2007.
126. A.D. interview, 13 April 2007.
127. D.R. and A.D. interviews, April 2007.
128. F.D. interview, 13 April 2007.
129. J.L. interview, 18 April 2007.
130. A.W. numerous interviews.
131. G.T. interview, 12 April 2007.
132. B.W. interview, 19 April 2007.
133. O.R. interview, 16 April 2007.
134. H.F. interview, 22 June 2007.
135. Albert Rigby. Imperial War Museum: Papers of Mr A.Rigby and many interviews and conversations. I came across Albert's writing in the Imperial war Museum when I was researching the Second World War and Colwyn Bay. Later, my school friend suggested I interview her godparents and to our amazement it turned out that they were Albert and his wife. Since then I have visited them in their home, read the books they have written and had many telephone conversations. Here Albert remembers the war years and his memories of the town as an eighteen-year old. Sadly he has now passed away.
136. P.B. interview, 19 April 2007.
137. P.B. has since told me that a landscape painting survived the bombing, and still hangs in her house to this day.
138. Author's experience.
139. G.R. interview, 17 April 2007
140. D.B. interview, 19 April 2007
141. Census prepared by the Office of National Statistics, Hampshire. By e-mail census. customerservice@ons.gsi.gov.uk, on 6 July 2007.
142. B.D. was found at the same Scout centenary as Hans Wins, and she was recognised from the days when the author's brother was a scout and B.D. an Akela. On arrival at B.D.'s house for the interview, her sister in law, M.H. was waiting too, as both had worked for the Ministry during wartime.
143. This can be found on a website www.conwyscoutsassociation.org.uk, click heritage and see item eleven.
144. It would most likely have contained rough cuttable, as well as diamonds in various stages of cuttings taken from the factory in a hurry, industrial and polished, finished diamonds.
145. He also asked the author if she could use the sawing machine as he wanted to cut some diamonds!
146. H.W. interviews.
147. G.R. interview, 17 April 2007.
148. H.W. numerous interviews.

## 7: Contributions from civil servants from other areas of the UK during the war

149. Coal miners and engineers in Saundersfoot.
150. From the *Surrey Comet* newspaper, 12 June 1954.
151. Sir Jack Drummond (1891–1952). A lecture series at Queen Mary University is dedicated to him. He pioneered research on vitamins in the 1930s and played a key role during the Second World War in advising Lord Woolton at the Ministry of Food about vitamin supplements to rations. He was given a knighthood for his contributions in this area.
152. Olwen had never heard of the term 'Guinea Pigs' until she passed on details to her sister-in-law Elizabeth.
153. By 1942, 217,000 women were serving in the ATS.

## 8: The War

154. B.W. and D.B. interview, 19 April 2007.
155. F.D. information.
156. J.L. interview, 18 April 2007.
157. D.B. interview, 19 April 2007.

## 9: Developments and impact

158. G.T. interview, 12 April 2007.
159. P.B. interview, 12 April 2007.
160. A. Marwick, *War and Social Change in the Twentieth Century*, Macmillan, London, 1974, p.151.
161. J.L. interview, 18 April 2007.
162. Wallis, Jill A Welcome in the Hillside? (Wirral : Avid. 2000)
163. *North Wales Weekly News*, 7 January 1940: 'There is alarm at the monoglot English children. Plans to give instructions in Welsh. Financial and cultural loss to Wales'.
164. J. Graham Jones, *The History of Wales*, University of Wales Press, Cardiff, 1990, p.144.
165. A. Marwick, *War and Social Change in the Twentieth Century*, Macmillan, London, 1974, p.156.
166. ibid, p.155.
167. G.T. interview, 12 April 2007.
168. ibid.
169. ibid.
170. J. Davies, A History of Wales, Penguin, UK, 1994, p.600, quoted in J. Wallis, *A Welcome in the Hillside?*.
171. A. Marwick, *War and Social Change in the Twentieth Century*, Macmillan, London, 1974, p.160.
172. J. Graham Jones, *The History of Wales*, University of Wales Press, Cardiff, 1990, p.145.
173. Census prepared by the Office of National Statistics. Hampshire. By e-mail census.customerService@ons.gsi.gov.uk, 6 July 2007.
174. Oral history, verified by editorials.
175. G. Edwards, The Borough of Colwyn Bay. A Social History 1934–1974, Colwyn Borough Council, 1984, p.38.
176. ibid.
177. D.B. interview, 19 April 2007.

178. B.W. interview, 19 April 2007.
179. G. E. Mellor, Colwyn Bay Cricket Club. A Club History, Rhos Press, Rhos, 1992.
180. G. Edwards, The Borough of Colwyn Bay. A Social History 1934–1974, Colwyn Borough Council, 1984, p.37.
181. G. Edwards, The Borough of Colwyn Bay. A Social History 1934–1974, Colwyn Borough Council, 1984, p.29.

**10: 'Opportunity or Menance?' does the town now deserve credit and reparation?**
182. Title of a survey on evacuation by Department of Social Science, University of Liverpool, quoted in article in the *North Wales Weekly News*, 14 March 1940.
183. D.B. interview, 17 April 2007.
184. For example, Land Girls have recently been acknowledged for their contribution.
185. Captain Harry Parker, RA, retired schoolmaster at Pendorlan and Eirias High School.

# Bibliography

Every effort has been made to seek owners of copyright material and to request permission.

## Primary Sources: Unpublished
*Official Documents*
   National Archives, Kew, London (TNA)
      Papers of the Ministry of Food:
         MAF 83/945 Liaison arrangements with other government departments.
         MAF 72/58 Population figures.
         MAF 102/60 Work of the MoF 102/55 Report commissioned.
         MAF 127/275. Communications and facilities.
         Suspect List HO45/25569. These were closed until 2000.

## Private papers
   Denbighshire Record Office, Ruthin:
      Papers and photographs from Braids Garage (DD/DM/1175/)1
      Papers of the Ministry of Works:
      Requisitioning of buildings. Secret (DD/PO/481)
   Imperial War Museum:
      Papers of Albert Rigby (94/6/1 1990)
      Papers of Mr A. F. Ebert, MBE (78/68/1)
      The diary of Captain Cutler. Lent by his daughter Vicky Cutler.

## Parish Records
   Marriage certificates at St Paul's and St John's from 1939 to 1945, on microfilm at Colwyn Bay Library. Database of author.

## Letters and e-mails.
   Margaret Harvey (née Lloyd)
   Geoff Parselle

Dr John Wainwright
Mairwen Roberts
Marjorie MacAleese
Olwen Hughes (née Dodd)
Elizabeth.
Audrey Andrew
F.D. from Essex

**Oral Testimony**
*Interviews*
Derek Bellis, 19 April 2007; Peggy Bowden, 19 April 2007; Betty Dale and Margaret Holtham, 11 June 2008; Aline and Fred Davies, 13 April 2007; Helen Finch, 22 June 2007; June Lee, 18 April 2007; Captain Harry Parker, 22 June 2007; Albert Rigby, 25 June 2007; Diana and David Roberts, 20 June 2007; Glen Roberts, 17 April 2007; Olive Roberts, 16 April 2007; G.T., 12 April 2007; Brian Whittingham, 19 April 2007; Alan Wheway, 20 June 2007; Hans Wins, 23 June 2007.

*Telephone interviews*
Wynne Jones 23 July 2007; Neville Whale 22 June 2007.

**Primary Sources: Published**
*Newspapers*
   *North Wales Weekly News*, 1939–45, on microfilm at Colwyn Bay Library.
*Memoirs*
   Woolton, Lord Frederick. *Memoirs of the Earl of Woolton* (Cassell: 1959).

**Secondary Sources**
*Books*
Caunce, S., *Oral History and the Local Historian* (London & New York: Longman: 1994).
Chambers Jones, R., *Bless 'Em All* (Wrexham: Bridge Books, 1995).
Edwards, G., *The Borough of Colwyn Bay. A Social History, 1934–1974*. (Colwyn Borough Council: 1984).
Felton, M., *Civilian Supplies in Wartime Britain*. (IWM: Reprinted 2003).
Hughes, M., *Conwy Mulberry Harbour* (Llanrwst: Gwasg Carreg Gwalch, 2001).

Graham Jones, J., *The History of Wales* (Cardiff: University of Wales Press, 1990).
Marwick, A., *War and Social Change in the Twentieth Century* (Hampshire: Macmillan, 1974).
Mellor, G. E., *Colwyn Bay Cricket Club, A Club History* (Rhos: Rhos Press, 1992).
Summerfield, P. and Peniston Bird, C., *Contesting Home Defence* (Manchester: Manchester University Press, 2007).
Tosh J., *Pursuit of History* (London: Longman, 2002).
Tucker, N. and Wynne Jones, I., *Colwyn Bay Its History Across the Years* (Derbyshire: Landmark, 2001).
Walker, David E., *Operation Amsterdam* (Herts: Mayflower, 1974).
Wallis, Jill, *A Welcome in the Hillside?* (Wirral: Avid. 2000).
Williams, John R., *No 1 Battalion (Denbighshire) Home Guard* (Colwyn Bay: R. E. Jones & Bros Ltd).
Wynne Jones, Ivor, *Hitler's Celtic Echo* (Llandudno: Pegasus. 2006).

*Internet*
www.conwyscoutsassociation.org.uk
http://www.subbrit.org.uk/rsg/features/government/
http://www.arts.manchester.ac.uk/subjectareas/history/research/cchw/research/contestinghomedefence/
Operation Kindertransport
http://www.gwrychtrust.co.uk/html/operation_kindertransport.html
Rhydymwyn Storage Site
http://www.rvsweb.org.uk/ourhistory.htmlAShortHistory 10 April 2007
Census Office of National statistics Hampshire

*By e-mail*
census.customercervice@ons.gsi.gov.uk 6 July 2007.

---

**Please contribute**

If you have any memories of Colwyn Bay which we can record, please contact the author via Bridge Books or through Eunice Roberts at Colwyn Bay Library.